LILLIAN
HELLMAN

LILLIAN
HELLMAN

REBEL PLAYWRIGHT

RUTH TURK

Lerner Publications Company/Minneapolis

To my loving children, Barbara and Richard.
Thanks for always being there for me.

Library of Congress Cataloging-in-Publication Data

Turk, Ruth
  Lillian Hellman, rebel playwright / by Ruth Turk.
    p.   cm.
  Includes index.
  ISBN 0-8225-4921-2
  1. Hellman, Lillian, 1905–1984—Biography—Juvenile literature.
2. Women dramatists, American—20th century—Biography—
Juvenile literature. [1. Hellman, Lillian, 1905–1984. 2. Authors,
American. 3. Women—Biography.] I. Title.
PS3515.E343Z945 1995
812'.52—dc20   94-27060

Manufactured in the United States of America

1 2 3 4 5 6 – I/JR – 00 99 98 97 96 95

Contents

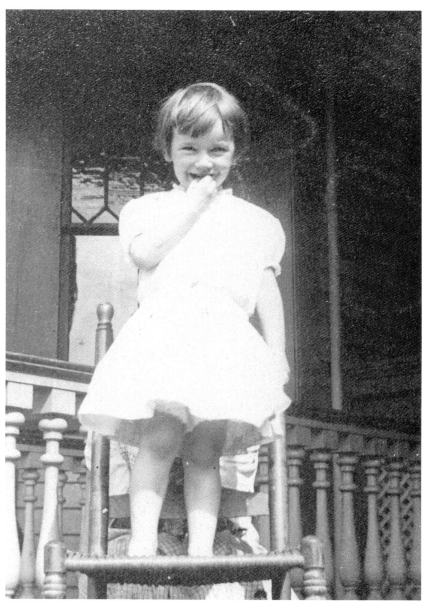

Lillian Hellman at age three

ONE

The Fig Tree

1905–1913

"I suppose I was eight or nine before I discovered the pleasures of the fig tree, and although I have lived in many houses since then, including a few I made for myself, I still think of it as my first and most beloved home."
—Lillian Hellman, *An Unfinished Woman*

On a warm, lazy day in New Orleans, eight-year-old Lillian Hellman sat up in bed and listened to the sounds floating up the back stairs. The clink of dishes and rattle of pots and pans did not drown out the voices of the boarders around the breakfast table. Aunt Jenny and Aunt Hannah had been up for hours baking and cooking. Lillian could pick out their bubbly voices laughing and joking back and forth with Mr. Stillman and the others as if they didn't have a care in the world. She sighed. She wished she could be more like her jolly aunts, especially Jenny, the prettier one. She liked living with her parents in her aunts' boardinghouse on Prytania Street, but she didn't understand how her aunts could stand cooking for a bunch of people who weren't family. Lillian didn't mind that Jenny and Hannah never asked her to get up early to help with the boarders.

Lillian spent hours daydreaming and reading in her favorite fig tree.

Lillian had plans of her own for today, starting with skipping breakfast. Moving quickly, she washed and dressed, putting on the flowered cotton dress and polished black shoes her mother had laid out for her to wear. She pulled on the floppy hat with the long ribbons she hated, knowing that as soon as she was out of sight of the house she would take it off.

Today was the second day this week she was skipping school. Still, she would act like she was on the way to school in case anyone should ask. Because she was far ahead in all her subjects, Lillian knew she would not be missing much. Nobody ever checked attendance and Lillian felt confident no one would find out. Max Hellman, Lillian's father, had already left the house to look for work. Her mother, Julia, liked to sleep late. Lillian was careful to move softly so as not to wake her in the next room.

Swinging her school bag over her shoulder, the young girl tiptoed down the stairs and stopped outside the kitchen door. Every morning Aunt Jenny prepared a lunch basket for Lillian, knowing that her niece didn't want to come into the kitchen and have to talk to all the boarders. Lillian wanted to thank her aunt for the delicious goodies she knew were inside, but the thought of Mr. Stillman and Sarah and Fizzy fussing over her made her move even faster. It wasn't that she didn't like older people. She just liked being alone a lot more. Today she was going to have a day by herself—no parents, no teachers, not even other children.

But first she needed to go through all the motions of starting out for school. For the benefit of neighbors who were out on their front porches, Lillian walked to the corner of St. Charles Avenue and sat on a bench, pretending to wait for a streetcar.

As soon as the neighbors moved indoors to take their after-breakfast naps, Lillian put her morning plan into action. Taking off her hat, she tied the ribbons together and slipped them around her neck. A warm breeze tugged at loose strands of the girl's reddish-blond hair, which she pushed behind her ears. In a little while she reached the banks of the Mississippi River.

Although she enjoyed watching the children swimming in the muddy water, she had no desire to join them. As an only child, Lillian was used to doing things by herself. Sometimes she liked being with other people, but most of the time she enjoyed her own company and rarely felt lonely. It was fun watching what was happening around her even if she wasn't a part of it. Sometimes she liked to watch the parades that would come marching down Canal Street.

The sun rose higher in the sky and the air grew muggy. Lillian hiked up her dress and sat down on the curb. On the corner, the hurdy-gurdy man strummed out lively tunes, cranking the handle on the little organ while Lillian hummed the music under her breath. Cajun vendors hawked their wares to the busy housewives out doing their daily shopping. Soon a friendly "white wing" came down the street. (In the early 1900s in New Orleans, the people who cleaned the streets were called white wings because they wore white jackets.) The white wing smiled at the little girl on the curb. Lillian thought his teeth were whiter than his uniform. When he said good morning she opened her lunch basket and held it out to him. She offered him one of Aunt Jenny's fried chicken legs, but he shook his head, explaining that he could not eat on the job. Then he touched his forehead with his hand in a polite gesture and, still smiling, moved on down the street. Lillian couldn't see how nibbling a fried chicken leg would interfere with cleaning the street. She could eat her aunt's mouthwatering chicken any time at all!

Lillian decided it was time to sneak back to the yard of her house. By now the boarders would be gone either to work, to shop, or to take naps, so it would be quiet around the house on Prytania Street. Her aunts and Carrie, the cook, would still be busy in the kitchen, but they wouldn't bother to look up into the old fig tree. The fig tree was only a few feet from the house, but three live oak trees hid it. Enclosed in the fig tree's thick branches, Lillian felt safe and secure in a secret world of her own.

She had managed to make her leafy hideout a most comfortable spot. She had a sling to hold her schoolbag, a pulley

Streetcars were a common form of transportation in early 20th-century New Orleans.

rope to hoist up the lunch basket, a fishing pole in case she decided to do a little fishing later on, a pillow, and a nail to hold her dress and shoes, keeping them neat for her return to the house.

Up in the tree, Lillian stripped to her underwear and chose a book to read. Inside the pages of a book was yet another world to explore. The words were not always easy to understand because Lillian usually read books that were quite advanced for her age. She found that the adults in the stories were usually different from the kind of people she knew in everyday life. In the books Lillian read, the characters spoke perfectly, wore elegant clothes, and had the most exciting adventures.

Young Lillian could watch riverboats—such as this steamer loaded with cotton—traveling up and down the Mississippi.

The hours passed quickly as the girl in the tree kept turning the pages. She ignored the growing afternoon heat. When she felt hungry, she nibbled on a chicken leg, a juicy peach, or a piece of rich chocolate cake. When her eyelids began to droop, she closed them and rested her head on the pillow.

After a short nap, Lillian slipped back into her dress. Carrying her fishing pole, she climbed down from the tree. In the next street, water from the Gulf of Mexico flowed in a narrow trench alongside the gutter, bringing all sorts of things, including fresh fish. Dangling her fishing pole, Lillian hunched down and fished in the trench. Usually she caught a crab or a crayfish, but even if there was nothing much to catch, fishing was a pleasant change of pace in the long afternoon. Lillian always went back to her reading afterward. That was one of the wonderful things about reading a book. She could be sure the characters would always be there even if she left them for a while.

Lillian was born on June 20, 1905. At the age of eight, she liked to do things her own way, and a leisurely afternoon in her secret hideaway was a perfect way to show her independence. She was already a rebel.

Six-year-old Lillian poses for a photographer

TWO

New Orleans

1913–1919

"I was born in New Orleans to Julia Newhouse from Demopolis, Alabama, who had fallen in love and stayed in love with Max Hellman, whose parents had come to New Orleans in the German 1845–1848 immigration to give birth to him and his two sisters."

—Lillian Hellman, *An Unfinished Woman*

Because he couldn't find permanent work in New Orleans, Max Hellman tried to make a fresh start in New York. Lillian and her mother spent six months of the year in New Orleans and six in an apartment on the Upper West Side of New York. As Lillian grew older, she had a rough time adjusting to the frequent moves. Sometimes Max's search for work took him away from home. Though she missed her father, in Lillian's eyes he was a hero. Lillian's mother, Julia, had defied her own parents to marry Max. Julia's parents wanted her to marry a wealthy man, but Julia was in love with Max. Max's two sisters, Hannah and Jenny, adored and looked up to him. They loved waiting on their brother when he was home, cooking and fussing over his favorite dishes.

Lillian's aunts taught her to cook in the house on Prytania Street. Every Sunday it was her job to clean the crayfish for New Orleans bisque. Aunt Jenny and Carrie, the cook, also taught Lillian to make turtle soup and to pluck and cook the wild ducks that were usually served for Sunday dinner. Besides providing a dozen or more boarders with their wonderful New Orleans-style cooking every day, Lillian's aunts fed homeless men, women, and children—black and white—who came to the back door. No one was ever turned away. Many poor people lived in the city, and on most nights after dinner, the back porch became a pretty busy place.

In 1913 New Orleans was a segregated city. This meant that black people were banned from using the same restaurants, theaters, parks, and public restrooms as white people. Facilities for blacks were usually inferior.

At an early age, Lillian had a black nanny named Sophronia Mason. The little girl went everywhere with her adored nanny, sitting with her in the back of the streetcar in the section reserved for blacks. Being so young, Lillian didn't question this situation at first.

Then one day things changed. Lillian saw Max Hellman help a black girl who was being taunted and harassed by a group of white boys. Lillian was very moved and impressed by her father's action. The next time she entered a streetcar with her nanny, she tried to take things into her own hands.

Instead of following Sophronia to the back of the streetcar, Lillian tried to push her into a seat behind the white driver. While the driver glared at them, Sophronia grabbed the little girl's hand and started moving toward the back of the bus. Suddenly Lillian felt tears spring to her eyes. She felt as if her nanny did not understand what she was trying to do.

This New Orleans restaurant only served blacks. Others served whites only. As a child, Lillian was disturbed by the unfairness of segregation.

In a panic, Lillian stumbled out of the trolley and ran down the street. Sophronia followed. When she finally caught Lillian, she scolded the child lovingly but firmly. She explained that it was wrong to give in to her feelings without thinking how it could upset other people. Lillian loved her nanny, but she disagreed. Sophronia told her that a little girl could not change things, but Lillian wouldn't believe her. She wanted to be independent and be able to change things. She couldn't wait to grow up.

Lillian befriended some of the children who lived in this orphanage on Prytania Street.

Lillian idolized her father as much as his sisters did. She considered Max Hellman to be handsome, funny, and bright—much more exciting than her mother, who seemed quiet and mousy by contrast. But one day while walking down Jackson Avenue, a horrified Lillian saw Max Hellman embrace Fizzy, one of her aunts' boarders, and kiss her soundly on the lips. Then the two of them climbed into a waiting taxi and drove away. For a long moment Lillian stood there staring after the departing cab. The idea of her father being unfaithful to her mother made her miserable. She wanted to kill Max and Fizzy. Instead she ran all the way home. Climbing into her beloved fig tree, she flung herself headlong to the ground—resulting in a broken nose. Lillian Hellman had a crooked profile for the rest of her life.

Although Lillian's image of her father was never the same, Aunt Jenny and Aunt Hannah continued to be two of her favorite relatives. Lillian especially looked forward to Saturday night outings with Aunt Hannah—going to the movies, then to the French Quarter, where they browsed in secondhand bookstores. Hannah bought her niece old leather-bound books and magazines with yellow pages and no covers. Some of this reading material was perfect for the hours spent up in the fig tree. Lillian also loved listening to the stories Aunt Hannah told about her childhood and about the Hellman grandparents who died before Lillian was born.

Another place where Lillian spent a lot of time was in an orphanage down the block from the boardinghouse. She made friends with some of the kids who lived there, finding them more interesting than her classmates in school. In Lillian's eyes, the independence of being an orphan seemed desirable.

Among her friends in the orphanage was a pretty girl named Frances who liked to boast that her father was killed by the Mafia. A girl named Miriam kept stealing money from Lillian's purse and beat her up when she protested. Pancho, an orphan with dark, sad eyes, told Lillian in Spanish that he loved her. All that night she could not sleep because of this declaration.

Once, when she was about 14, Lillian went to a Catholic mass with Pancho and a boy named Louis Calda. Lillian was so impressed by the unfamiliar ceremony that she felt she could have converted from Judaism. When Louis told her he did not think she was worthy, Lillian burst into tears. To stop her from crying, Pancho cut off a lock of his hair and gave it to her as a gift. Lillian was quite moved. She went home and put the lock of hair in the back of a new wristwatch her father had given her for her birthday. The next day the watch stopped working.

Max Hellman was very upset when he learned the watch was not working. He insisted on taking it back to the jeweler immediately. Lillian did not explain about the hair. A few days later, Max, embarrassed that the jeweler hadn't actually been at fault, yelled at his daughter. He demanded to know why she hadn't told him about the hair. Lillian paled, but she refused to answer. In front of all the boarders, Mr. Hellman continued shouting and scolding the shaking girl until he was nearly hoarse. Julia Hellman left the room and the aunts went out on the porch. They all felt sorry for Lillian, but they realized there was no use trying to stop Max Hellman when his temper reached the boiling point.

By the time Max finished his outburst, Lillian felt sick. When her father finally dismissed her, she fled to her room and threw up out the window. Early the next morning, she got dressed, grabbed her purse and, sneaking out of the house, walked a long way down St. Charles Avenue. She wasn't sure where she was going or what she would do when she got there.

Lillian walked until she came to the railroad station. A thought came to her. Maybe she could get on a train and travel far away. She stood in line at the ticket window to ask where she could go for four dollars, which was all she had. But when she got to the window she lost her nerve and walked away.

Toward evening, tired and hungry, Lillian found herself in the French Quarter. She bought half a loaf of bread and some Tootsie Rolls, then sat on the steps of St. Louis Cathedral and ate. The night was damp and hot, and she soon dozed off. She was awakened by unfamiliar stomach cramps. She went back to the railroad station and into the ladies' room. She washed her face with cold water but when she looked in the mirror her skin was pale and blotched. Now Lillian was really frightened. Between the cramps and the way she looked, she felt like something strange was happening to her. She needed to find a place to lie down and rest, but she didn't want to go home.

Lillian kept wandering until finally she came to a black neighborhood that seemed familiar. She recognized the streets because Sophronia used to take her to a dressmaker there who made her pretty dresses. The dressmaker wasn't there anymore, but Lillian went up and down the block until she saw a house with a sign that said "Rooms for Rent." At first no one would rent a room to a young girl.

New Orleans's Old French Market

The night that Lillian ran away from home, she napped on the steps of the famous St. Louis Cathedral.

Then Lillian thought of saying she was related to Sophronia Mason because she knew that Sophronia and her family were respected in the black community of New Orleans. Finally, a woman rented a room to Lillian for two and a half dollars. Scared and exhausted, the girl lay down on the bed and fell fast asleep.

After sleeping for hours, she woke and saw a man standing at the foot of the bed. It was Max Hellman. Behind him stood Sophronia. Lillian's father told her to get up and get dressed, but she began crying and told him she couldn't. Mr. Hellman left the room and Lillian tried to explain to her nanny. Sophronia looked at her and said, "Get you going or I will never see you whenever again."

Lillian stared at her. She knew she would keep her word. The thought that she might never see beloved Sophronia again was too much to bear. Dressing quickly, she went down the stairs and out to the street, where her father was waiting. They didn't speak. Together with Sophronia they walked to the streetcar line. When the trolley came, the black woman nodded good-bye to the father and daughter. Then she climbed aboard and took a seat in the back. Before she did, Lillian caught a glimpse of Sophronia's face turned in her direction. Sophronia smiled gently, and Lillian knew the smile was for her.

Max Hellman and his daughter went to Vanalli's Restaurant, a popular place for dinner. Lillian's father ordered a big meal even though she told him she wasn't hungry. Finally he asked her if she wanted him to apologize and Lillian said yes, she did. After Max's apology, Lillian proceeded to eat everything her father had ordered, including crayfish, grilled fish with Bernaise sauce, french fries, and even a small steak.

Lillian ate every bit of food, then started to mumble under her breath.

"God forgive me, Papa forgive me, Mama forgive me, Sophronia, Jenny...."

"You're talking to yourself," said Lillian's father. "I can't hear you. What are you saying?"

Lillian repeated the prayer. Her father laughed and said, "Where do you start your training as the first Jewish nun on Prytania Street?"

Now it was Lillian's turn to laugh. I like my father again, she thought. Maybe Papa was not really so awful. She told him about her painful cramps and the start of her menstrual period. Max Hellman stared at his daughter. Then he took her hand and said it was time to go home to Lillian's mother.

It had been a long, tiring day. Running away was not a pleasant experience, but Lillian felt more independent somehow, almost as if she had won a battle.

Lillian Hellman as a young woman

THREE

New York

1919–1924

> "But that New York apartment where we visited several times a week, the summer cottage where we went for a visit each year as the poor daughter and granddaughter, made me into an angry child and forever caused in me a wild extravagance mixed with respect for money and those who have it."
> —Lillian Hellman, *An Unfinished Woman*

Until Lillian was 16 years old, the Hellmans continued to move back and forth from New Orleans to New York. The apartment on West 95th Street in Manhattan seemed small and crowded compared to the rambling boardinghouse in New Orleans. It was a frustrating time for a girl accustomed to open spaces, tall trees, and a backyard. Although Max Hellman eventually found a good job as a traveling salesman, Lillian continued to think of her family as poor for a long time.

Living in a congested neighborhood where trees and backyards were rare was not the worst part of life in New York for Lillian. The worst part was visiting her grandmother every week. Sophie Newhouse, Julia Hellman's mother, lived in an elegant townhouse not far from the Hellmans' apartment.

Sophie was a widow, but she shared her home with her brother Jacob as well as two of her unmarried daughters.

To Lillian, everything about the Newhouse residence seemed dull and stuffy. The many rooms were cluttered with valuable antiques and ornate furniture, but this made little impression on the young girl.

Sunday dinner in particular was an ordeal. Lillian dreaded sitting at the big table surrounded by pompous, loud adults who kept talking over and around her about things she knew little about.

Sometimes Sophie gave parties for Lillian's great-aunts, uncles, and other relatives. Whenever possible, Lillian managed to escape to the servants' hall where she could watch the goings-on through a crack in the door.

Sometimes Lillian felt as if she were at a circus, except that the events weren't very amusing. Dinner was often like a big business meeting, and Sophie was always in charge. The topic of conversation was always money—who had the most money, who spent too much of it, and who would inherit what. This made Lillian angry and unhappy, because not having much money of their own, her parents were often left out of the discussion. She began to develop a feeling of inferiority mixed with awe for people who did have a lot of money.

At Public School 6 in Manhattan, Lillian's attendance was not much better than it had been in school in New Orleans, but for different reasons. While she could easily stay ahead in her classwork in New Orleans, in New York she had trouble keeping up. Moving back and forth made it difficult for Lillian to be a good student. But trouble in school did not keep her from reading all the books she could get her hands on. Through books, she could escape from a world she sometimes found hard to understand.

Lillian and her parents lived on Manhattan's Upper West Side (right), where she attended Public School 6 (below).

Lillian also escaped through adventures with her best friend, Helen Schiff. During freezing weather, the two girls sometimes cut classes and went for walks along the ice-covered Hudson River. After coming back to the Schiffs' apartment, Lillian often lit up a cigarette, only to toss it out the open window when Helen's mother entered the room. Eventually the school principal called Mrs. Schiff and warned her that Lillian Hellman was a bad influence on Helen.

Lillian's vivid imagination led her into all sorts of adventures. In 1917 the United States was fighting Germany in World War I. Lillian had been reading newspaper accounts about spies, so she decided that she and Helen would track down German spies who might be slinking through the streets of Manhattan. One afternoon, the girls spotted two men in raincoats, one of whom was carrying a black violin case. Lillian imagined a dangerous machine gun hidden inside the case. Immediately the girls rushed over to a police officer and reported the strangers as German spies. When the suspicious-looking characters turned out to be a college professor and a concert violinist, Lillian was more disappointed than embarrassed.

By the age of 14, Lillian was moody and defiant. Sometimes she challenged her father's orders just to see what would happen. When Mr. Hellman imposed a curfew of eleven o'clock, Lillian went out with a 19-year-old college student and did not return until well past midnight. When her father grew furious with her, she called on the college student and asked him to take care of her. Instead, the young man politely but firmly escorted her back home.

In 1918 Lillian entered the Wadleigh High School in Manhattan. She described it as "a large, smelly dump where I was taught nothing. I spent a good deal of my spare time looking up naughty words in the dictionary." Her best subjects were

Lillian graduated from Manhattan's Wadleigh High School.

English and history. She never received more than a 70 in math. For a while, she tried her hand at writing a column for the school paper. She called it "It Seems to Me, Jr." after the popular column "It Seems to Me" by journalist Heywood Broun. She also tried acting in a school play called *Mrs. Gorringe's Necklace,* a mystery thriller. Lillian was assigned the villain's part, a minor role that the young actress made the most of. When a stuck door prevented her from making an exit, Lillian didn't panic, but remained on stage, utterly relaxed, making casual, completely original remarks. A few minutes later the horrified drama coach managed to fix the door and wave the villain backstage, but not before the audience broke into an appreciative round of applause.

When Lillian entered New York University in 1922, the Washington Square branch took up one floor of a six-story office building near Washington Square Park (above).

In 1922, a month before her 17th birthday, Lillian Hellman graduated from Wadleigh High School. Although Lillian did not like her mother's family, she had an interesting relationship with her uncle Jake. Jake gave Lillian a ring for graduation. But Lillian did not care for jewelry. She went to a pawnshop and hocked the ring for 25 dollars. With the money, she bought an armful of something much more important to her—books. A little while later, she decided to tell Uncle Jake what she had done. He stared at her for a long time. Then he laughed and said, "So you've got spirit after all. Most of the rest of them are made of sugar water."

Lillian's mother wanted her to attend Sophie Newcomb College in New Orleans where she had been a student, but Lillian wanted to go to Smith College, a prestigious women's college in Massachusetts. Her father decided he could not afford an expensive school, so Lillian entered the Washington Square branch of New York University.

Disappointed that she was unable to attend the college of her choice, Lillian did not make an enthusiastic student. Except for a few courses in literature and art, she found her classes dull. Once again she became restless. She began spending more time in the smoking lounge than going to class. At a time when students rarely left or skipped class, Lillian Hellman would walk out in the middle of a lecture by a prominent professor. She did this less to be rude than because she felt she was not in the place she wanted to be. Frequently the remainder of the day was spent in a Greenwich Village café nearby called Lee Chumley's. Lillian would curl up in a corner with a book or enter into a conversation with another patron. She claimed, "I was sometimes more advanced but often less educated than other students and I had little desire to be shown up."

Lillian had a sharp mind, but she lacked discipline. In her junior year, feeling that she was wasting time, Lillian dropped out of college. But leaving school did not mean she was short of ambition.

To celebrate Lillian's 19th birthday, Mrs. Hellman took her daughter on a trip through the Midwest and the South. When they returned, Lillian decided to search for a job, but she had no notion of where to start or what to look for. With her formal education incomplete, she was hardly qualified for the kind of job that might hold her interest.

Of medium height, with reddish-blond hair, a large nose, a keen expression, and a lively personality, Lillian exuded an air of confidence she did not always feel. Emerging from her teen years, she was still uncertain of her goals.

At the age of 19, Lillian left college to take a job in book publishing.

◀ FOUR ▶

Marriage
1924–1932

"I believed I was not doing or living the way I had planned. I had planned
nothing, of course. I was bewildered: if I really felt there were a million years
ahead of me, why then did I feel so impatient, so restless?"
—Lillian Hellman, *An Unfinished Woman*

In the autumn of 1924, Lillian attended a party and met
some important women and men, including Julian Messner,
vice president of a leading publishing house called Boni and
Liveright. Lillian had never met a publisher before. She fell
into a lengthy conversation with Mr. Messner, who listened
thoughtfully to everything the young woman said. By the end
of the evening, the publisher was so impressed with Lillian's
intelligence and knowledge of books that he offered her a job
doing general office work at Boni and Liveright. She was
delighted. But once on the job, she soon discovered the ups
and downs of working for Boni and Liveright.

One of the advantages of Lillian's new job was the contact
she had with a number of brilliant and talented writers. During the period Lillian worked there, Boni and Liveright

discovered and published authors such as William Faulkner, Ernest Hemingway, Eugene O'Neill, Sherwood Anderson, and Theodore Dreiser.

Boni and Liveright was located in a brownstone building on West 48th Street in Manhattan. A clubhouse atmosphere— editors, writers, publishers, and friends trooping in and out— filled the air. Boni and Liveright was incredibly generous to up-and-coming writers in need of advice, an advance on a manuscript, or possibly a few drinks. Lillian took a little while getting used to the socializing that seemed to go on at all hours. This was the Roaring Twenties—an era of fun, frivolity, and uninhibited behavior.

Charleston contests were a popular form of entertainment in the 1920s.

Horace Liveright, one of Lillian's employers

Most of her coworkers liked Lillian's alertness and wit. For her part, Lillian made a conscientious effort to blend into the publishing organization. She joined in the office parties and celebrations, but as the weeks and months went by, it dawned on her that her job didn't provide a real challenge. She resented having to file, type, and do clerical work, which she found boring. She did not enjoy a lot of manuscript reading and advertising work. Rather than reread material passed on to her by other manuscript readers, Lillian really wanted to discover exciting new writers herself. But whenever she recommended books she felt had promise, the publishers disagreed. They said the books would not sell, and selling was the most important thing. After work, Lillian tried to forget her frustration by dating a young writer named Arthur Kober.

*Lillian married Arthur
Kober in 1925.*

One day in June 1925, Lillian was shocked to discover she was pregnant by Arthur. She did not want pregnancy to force her into marriage. Though she knew that abortion was illegal, Lillian decided to find a doctor who would perform the procedure. This was a risky business in the twenties. She did not tell her parents she was planning to have an abortion.

Although Arthur Kober agreed to pay for the abortion, Lillian waited until he was out of town to have it done. Struggling to be independent, Lillian went on her own to a doctor on Coney Island who performed the operation without an anesthetic. After it was over, Lillian went home, weaker and more scared than she had expected to be.

The next morning she felt quite sick and exhausted. Worried that her mother would call a doctor and discover the reason for her sickness, she returned to work, hoping her condition would go unnoticed. Much to her anger and resentment, everyone looked at her sympathetically and asked how she felt. One of her employers, Horace Liveright, offered her a glass of champagne. Julian Messner invited her out to lunch. All of a sudden, Lillian was the center of the kind of attention she didn't want, and it made her miserable. Later she discovered that her coworker who had recommended the abortion doctor and promised to keep everything secret had leaked the news. Lillian was furious, but it was too late to do anything about it.

On December 31, 1925, Lillian Hellman and Arthur Kober were married. To all appearances, the Kobers seemed to make a well-matched couple. While their personalities were different, Arthur contributed much of the laughter and energy to the relationship that it needed. Most of the time, the young husband managed to have a soothing effect on his wife when she was going through a bad time. Lillian was impressed that Arthur wanted to be a professional writer and already showed promise. She liked the idea that he adored the theater. Arthur was determined to be a successful playwright—something he and Lillian had in common.

Both Lillian and Arthur were Jewish, but their backgrounds and upbringing were different. When Arthur was four years old, he and his family immigrated to the United States from Austria-Hungary. They lived in a crowded tenement on Manhattan's Lower East Side in a mostly Italian-Irish neighborhood. The Kobers had to share a bathroom with six other families. Arthur—along with a few other Jewish kids who lived in the area—had been frequently beaten up by the Italian and Irish kids who were often bigger and stronger.

Arthur overcame the tough times mostly because of his stamina, perseverance, and sense of humor. These same qualities served to get him through high school and into jobs as a bookkeeper for a real estate company, a stenographer, and a reviewer of vaudeville shows. Shortly before the wedding, Arthur became a press agent, arranging publicity for Broadway shows. He hoped to become a writer of screenplays and Broadway hits, but in 1925, the most notable event in his life was his marriage to the restless Lillian Hellman.

As soon as the Kobers returned from their honeymoon, Lillian grew even more restless. She asked her husband to help her make a job contact. The result was a position doing publicity for a Broadway revue called, "Bunk of 1926."

Unfortunately, the show closed soon after opening, but Lillian received her first taste of the theater. She sensed how exciting it could be, but she needed another opportunity to explore.

The next job to come along was writing book reviews for the *New York Herald Tribune*. Her name appeared in print for the first time. Unfortunately, assignments were only occasional, and the pay rate of $4.70 per column was not very rewarding.

A few months later, Arthur found a position in France as editor of a magazine called *The Paris Comet*. Lillian was thrilled at the thought of going with him. She could hardly wait to arrive in the glamorous city of Paris.

The Kobers stayed in a small hotel on Paris's Left Bank. They socialized with other Americans who were mostly interested in having a good time. The Left Bank of the Seine is an area famous for its artistic and intellectual activities. But instead of meeting writers and artists, the Kobers joined the other Americans, sight-seeing, eating and drinking at little sidewalk cafés, and complaining about how rudely the French

While living in Paris, Lillian and Arthur spent much of their time with other Americans in lively cafés such as this one.

treated Americans. While Arthur worked at his office, Lillian stayed home and wrote short stories, some of which were published in *The Paris Comet*. Dissatisfied with her own work, the author called them "lady-writer stories." She was not proud of them.

Before long, Lillian began to feel as aimless in Paris as she had in Manhattan. She grew to dislike the French city and looked for reasons to get away. Arthur encouraged his wife to take trips on her own, even helping to pay for them.

Delighted with Arthur's generosity, Lillian took off, traveling first to northern Italy. She found both the people and the scenery delightful. She also won enough money gambling in the casinos to extend her trip.

In 1927 the Kobers returned to the United States and moved into a house on Long Island. For a while, Lillian tried to play the role of suburban homemaker. She spent her time reading, playing bridge, and experimenting with the New Orleans cooking she remembered from her childhood. Occasionally she wrote a short story, but the results always left her dissatisfied. She didn't feel she had the ability to become a successful writer.

Seeing that she was unhappy, Arthur suggested that Lillian return to work. By now he realized she was not cut out to be a traditional, stay-at-home wife. Once again he found her a job, this time reading plays for the producer Anne Nichols. Nichols was among the few women playwrights and producers of that time. Unfortunately, Nichols's acting company failed, and Lillian again needed work.

She found a job doing publicity for a theater company in Rochester, New York. Since Kober's work as a Broadway press agent kept him in New York City, he was unable to go with his wife. The winter of 1928-29 was very cold, but Lillian remained in Rochester working, socializing, and playing bridge in the evenings. She was a skilled bridge player. In a few months she saved enough money from her winnings to afford a trip to Europe. Her marriage appeared to require less and less attention, and Arthur Kober accepted his wife's desire to travel.

Without a specific itinerary, Lillian roamed around Europe, enjoying the sights and the people. When she arrived in Germany, she stopped off at the University of Bonn. The pleasant atmosphere made her consider enrolling for courses and staying a while. At the university boardinghouse, she met a friendly group of students. They made her feel welcome, inviting her to parties and picnics.

One afternoon, during a discussion about politics, the students invited Lillian to join their youth organization. When they asked Lillian if she had any Jewish blood, she froze. Up

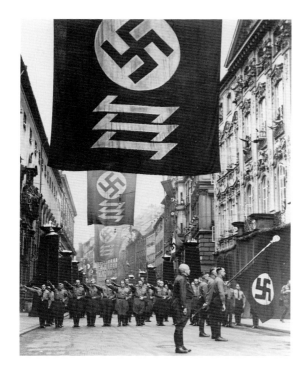

In the late 1920s, Adolf Hitler (seventh from left) *and the Nazi Party promoted anti-Semitism throughout Germany.*

until that moment she had not recognized that these friendly students were affiliated with the Nazis. In the summer of 1929, Adolf Hitler had begun to spread a wave of hatred and anti-Semitism throughout Germany. He wanted to establish himself as Germany's fuehrer (unquestioned leader) and make Germany the dominant world power. Hitler wanted to create a master race and tried to suppress all opposition to his beliefs. His plans included the torture and death of Jews and others who did not fulfill the requirements of his master plan.

In the United States, Lillian never had a reason to identify or explain her Jewishness. To her non-Jewish friends and acquaintances, Lillian's background had never been an issue. Now, it came as a shock that her ethnic heritage could affect

Lillian soon found life in glitzy Hollywood dull, despite the glamor of events such as movie premieres (above).

her life. "For the first time in my life, I thought about being a Jew." The next morning she packed and left Germany for home.

A few months after Lillian's return from Europe, Arthur was offered a job as a Hollywood screenwriter. In 1930 the American movie industry was experiencing a great surge of growth. The first talking pictures proved to be extremely successful, and attendance at movies increased rapidly. Another reason for the industry's growth was the country's slide into economic difficulties. People could forget about unemployment and the severe economic depression while watching the glamorous personalities on the silver screen. For many people, the movies served as a welcome means of escape from a drab existence and harsh reality.

To Arthur Kober, a screenwriter's salary of $450 a week was a terrific windfall. By Hollywood standards it was not impressive, but it was more money than Arthur and Lillian had ever seen. In the fall of 1930, they moved into an apartment in Hollywood. Once again, Lillian tried settling down, this time in the role of a Hollywood wife. This meant she sunbathed, played tennis, socialized, and joined in Hollywood's lively night life. She learned to stay up late and drink a lot like the rest of the crowd. But it wasn't long before her frustrating restlessness returned. She told her husband she hated the empty Hollywood routine. Once again, Arthur Kober tried to find a solution. He spoke to a story editor at the Metro-Goldwyn-Mayer studio. Soon, Lillian had a job as a script reader, evaluating screenplays for the studio.

Lillian wanted to write scripts, not read other people's, but she had little choice. Compared to her husband's salary, her own pay of $50 a week seemed pitifully low. She sat in a stuffy room with a dozen other readers, reviewing stories she usually thought were junk. Then she pounded out summaries on a rickety typewriter. The hours were long, and the work was boring. Lillian reacted by telling her fellow workers they should protest against their poor working conditions. When her employer found out she was trying to organize the others, he called her a troublemaker. Though Lillian had done a conscientious job of reviewing scripts, she was fired. Her boss felt that if Lillian managed to organize the other workers she could be dangerous. Losing this particular job did not upset Lillian, but she wished she could find a more exciting course to follow.

In the fall of 1930, Lillian sat in a Hollywood restaurant with her husband and a group of their friends. A tall, handsome

Lillian was attracted to handsome mystery writer Dashiell Hammett from the first moment she met him.

man entered the room. Lillian asked if anyone knew who he was. She was told that he was the famous detective-story writer, Dashiell Hammett. A few minutes later, Hammett approached the table and was introduced to everyone. Lillian could not take her eyes off the distinguished stranger. The attraction appeared mutual. To the astonishment of Arthur Kober and his friends, Lillian and Dashiell Hammett walked out of the restaurant together and sat in a parked car the rest of the evening. They talked mostly about books and writing.

Dashiell Hammett was a 36-year-old writer of detective fiction. His third novel, *The Maltese Falcon*, established him as one of the outstanding creators of modern thrillers. The hero of the book, Sam Spade, became the model for the "tough-guy" detective used by mystery writers for generations.

Born into a poor family in 1894, young Hammett had to leave school at the age of 13 in order to help with the family income. He took different jobs, including one as a salesclerk, another as a labor organizer. At the age of 20, he was employed as a detective for the famous Pinkerton Detective Agency. During World War I, he served in the army but was discharged when he contracted tuberculosis. For the next few years, Hammett was in and out of hospitals receiving treatment. In 1921, he fell in love with Josephine Dolan, one of his nurses. Hammett and Josephine married and had two children. But the mystery writer grew as restless in his marriage as Lillian Hellman had grown in hers. The Hammetts separated in 1929, and Josephine moved to Los Angeles with the children. Dashiell moved to Manhattan to concentrate on his writing career. When *The Maltese Falcon* brought wealth and recognition, Hammett moved from Manhattan to Hollywood.

After their restaurant encounter, Lillian and Dash started seeing a lot of each other, with Arthur Kober's full knowledge. Kober was a kind and gentle man who loved his wife. He tried to remain friends with both Lillian and Dash. He hoped the attraction between them would die out, but this never happened. In 1932, although Arthur and Lillian maintained an amicable relationship, they were divorced. Lillian and Dash moved to New York together.

Lillian at age 29

FIVE

A Playwright Is Born

1932–1936

"I decided a long time ago there were people who had to learn from other people. I'm one of them."

—Julie Rodman, *Days to Come*

Up until the time Dashiell Hammett came into her life, Lillian Hellman had trouble finding a sense of purpose or direction. She knew she wanted to write, but she didn't know how to begin.

With his sensitivity, brilliant mind, and blunt sense of humor, Dashiell Hammett turned out to be someone who could show Lillian the way to find a direction. Lillian was fascinated by the talented mystery writer, but she also respected him as a critic and a teacher. With Hammett's encouragement, Lillian experimented with writing humorous stories, two of which were published in *American Spectator* magazine. While this helped to bring her a reputation as a short story writer, her career soon took a different turn.

Writer Dorothy Parker and her husband, Alan Campbell, became close friends of Lillian's.

Lillian and Dash attended numerous literary gatherings. Lillian developed a friendship with novelist William Faulkner and became especially close to the witty writer, Dorothy Parker, who remained a friend for life. In 1933 at an elegant gathering in the home of composer Ira Gershwin, Lillian attracted the attention of Herman Shumlin, a successful Broadway producer. Impressed with Lillian's articulate conversation, Shumlin offered her a job as a play reader, much like her job reading screenplays. Knowing his reputation for putting on high-quality productions, she immediately accepted. As she read plays written by others, Lillian started thinking again about writing a play of her own. But where could she find material for an original plot or theme?

A comment made by Dash provided an answer. He had been reading a book about British court cases called *Bad Companions* by William Roughead. One of them was a story of two teachers in a girls' private school who were falsely accused of lesbianism by a student who disliked them. The women sued for libel—having one's reputation damaged. Although they won the case, their careers and personal lives were ruined.

Dash told Lillian he felt the story would make a powerful stage play. When Lillian hesitated, he added that if she didn't write the story, *he* would do it. Lillian believed him. She read the case for herself and decided it was exciting material for a play.

Herman Shumlin gave Lillian one of her first jobs in theater and eventually produced her first play.

In the spring of 1933, Lillian made notes and mulled over the plot and characters of her story. Dash finished writing *The Thin Man*, a novel that later became a hit Hollywood film. That summer Dash and Lillian rented a beach house on Long Island Sound, and Lillian tackled the first draft of her first play. She titled the play *The Children's Hour.*

With Dash's help, the play gradually began to unfold. Lillian wrote and rewrote scenes, changed lines, then changed them back again. Eventually there were 14 complete rewrites before she was satisfied. Though Dash offered important suggestions, his heavy drinking became a serious problem. Since meeting Dash, Lillian's own drinking had also increased. She realized

This famous publicity photo shows Dashiell Hammett arriving in Hollywood to write screenplays.

that unless she kept her drinking under control, her writing would suffer. Finally she decided it was necessary to do something drastic. She told Hammett she needed to concentrate. She was going to Paris to finish her play.

Dashiell Hammett was not upset. He realized Lillian needed privacy to accomplish her goal. He even provided the money for the trip. For more than two months Lillian lived alone in Paris, working on *The Children's Hour* until it was finished. She had never been able to exert this kind of discipline on herself before.

When Lillian returned from Paris with the completed script, she went to see her former boss, producer Herman Shumlin. When she did not find him in, she left the play on his desk with a note saying that in her opinion, this was the best script she had come across in all the time she had been reading for him.

Shumlin read the first act. Then he called Lillian and told her he agreed. After reading the entire play, he said he was ready to produce it. He started casting immediately and set up rehearsals.

On November 20, 1934, *The Children's Hour* opened on Broadway. It was a smash hit. While other women had written successful plays, few women had undertaken such a serious subject. At the time, most plays written by women were usually romances or light comedies.

Not everyone, however, was ready for Lillian's frank treatment of lesbianism. Some people were uncomfortable with or offended by the idea of a sexual relationship between two women. In 1935 members of the Pulitzer Prize Committee refused to consider the play for the best drama of 1934–35. This decision shocked actors, directors, producers, and theater critics. They had expected *The Children's Hour* to win a

Pulitzer. Angry over the injustice to Hellman's play, drama critics of major New York newspapers formed the Drama Critics Circle. They decided to present their own annual award.

In early 1935, plans were made to produce *The Children's Hour* in London, but because of its subject matter, the play was banned by British authorities. Undaunted, Shumlin managed to present the play at a private London theater club. At the end of that year, while the play was still showing to packed houses in New York, plans were made to present it in Boston and Chicago. Both cities banned the production. Despite these frustrations, *The Children's Hour* remained popular in New York, running for 691 performances. Soon Hollywood producers rushed to sign up the famous playwright.

Just three years before, Lillian had been a $50 a week reader at MGM. Now Samuel Goldwyn offered Hellman a contract to write screenplays for $60,000 a year. At that time only 10 percent of all screenwriters made more than $10,000 a year. Lillian Hellman found both financial and critical success. For the first time in her life, she was financially independent. She had gone from being unknown to international recognition.

Lillian and Dash rented a house in Hollywood. They made sure to find one large enough to give both of them privacy for writing. For her first screenwriting assignment, Lillian collaborated with a British writer on a movie called *Dark Angel*, a love story starring Merle Oberon and Fredric March. *Dark Angel* did well at the box office.

Now Lillian had total freedom to write about anything for her next screenplay. She chose to adapt *The Children's Hour.* At first, Sam Goldwyn worried about public reaction to the theme of lesbianism, but decided to ignore criticism.

Lillian, however, didn't want to face opposition from Hollywood censors. She chose a new title, *These Three.* While

Fredric March and Merle Oberon starred in the love story Dark Angel, *Lillian's first screenplay.*

keeping the basic idea and characters, she eliminated the lesbian relationship. In its place the author substituted a heterosexual romantic triangle. Lillian needed a great deal of talent and flexibility to reshape the plot, but she handled it skillfully. The film received rave notices. One review claimed that the stirring movie was not only worthy of the Broadway play but in some ways surpassed it.

Lillian adapted The Children's Hour *into* These Three, *an acclaimed film starring* (from left) *Merle Oberon, Joel McCrea, and Miriam Hopkins.*

Although Lillian had achieved great professional success, her personal life was far from smooth. On November 30, 1935, Lillian's mother died. While Julia Hellman was alive, she and Lillian had not been close. After Julia's death, Lillian realized how much she had loved her mother. She recognized that although Julia Hellman was a small, fragile woman, she was brave and sturdy in character.

Lillian also had to cope with Dash's growing drinking problem. When he stayed sober, he was gentle and caring. When he drank, however, he became irresponsible and even abusive. Sometimes Lillian ended up with a bruise or a black eye, but she never admitted to anyone how it happened. She tried unsuccessfully to persuade Dash to cut back on his drinking. Lillian found it increasingly difficult to write.

Finally she felt she had to leave him and return to New York. She rented an apartment and commuted between Manhattan and Hollywood, seeing Dash in his sober periods but leading a more independent life.

In the early 1930s, a growing economic depression began to affect the country. To help Hollywood studios cut costs, screenwriters were forced to take wage cuts. In 1934, one-third of all screenwriters earned less than $2,000 a year, had no job security between assignments, and had no control over their work. In other industries, workers around the United States were trying to organize into unions. They knew that unions, by fighting for workers' rights, would help to improve their economic conditions.

While Lillian was not financially affected by the Depression, she remained sympathetic to those who were. Lillian, along with Dashiell Hammett, Dorothy Parker, Theodore Dreiser, Robert Benchley, and other sympathetic writers, formed an organization called the Screen Writers' Guild. Like Lillian, those who were already successful did not have to be involved for financial security. And many successful writers did not want to place themselves at risk. They thought that joining a union might seem like disloyalty. Lillian went after the reluctant ones, urging them to join the guild and help improve working conditions for all writers.

At age 29, Lillian's success with The Children's Hour *brought her to Hollywood to work on screenplays.*

In 1936 Lillian wrote her second play. *Days to Come* focused on the struggle between labor and management. The play takes place in a small Midwestern town in the 1930s. A factory owner brings in strikebreakers in an effort to force laborers to return to work. When a strikebreaker is murdered in a drunken fight, a union organizer is blamed. As a result, the strikebreakers attack the workers, and a violent riot ensues in which the town is destroyed.

Days to Come opened on Broadway on December 15, 1936. During the first act, Hellman was so nervous she started drinking and threw up. She went home to change her clothes, and when she returned during the second act, she was shocked to see people leaving the theater. Despite its timely theme, *Days to Come* was a flop. Critics said the playwright had overloaded the story with too many situations and characters. After only six performances, the play closed.

Lillian was devastated, agonizing over the failure. She began to doubt her talent as a writer. Maybe the success of *The Children's Hour* had been a fluke. Should she give up writing or try harder the next time?

By the time she reached her early 30s, Lillian became known for her political activism as well as her writing.

◀ SIX ▶

Causes and Crusades

1936–1939

"All Fascists are not of one mind, one stripe. There are those who give the orders, those who carry out the orders, those who watch the orders being carried out. Then there are those who are half in, half hoping to come in. They are made to do the dishes and clean the boots."

—Kurt Muller, *Watch on the Rhine*

Lillian was diverted from the failure of *Days to Come* by a major political crisis. In July 1936, the Spanish civil war erupted—the result of a government takeover led by General Francisco Franco and his followers against President Manuel Azaña, leader of Spain's democratic government. Adolf Hitler and Benito Mussolini supported Franco. They wanted him to impose a fascist, or authoritarian government—similar to their repressive governments in Germany and Italy—in Spain. Only the Soviet Union helped the established government in Spain (the Loyalists) by sending advisers and weapons. Although no other countries gave their official support or aid, many individuals signed on as volunteers to help defend the Spanish republic. These volunteers were called the International Brigades.

They went to Spain to fight the fascists. Many gave their lives for this cause.

Lillian admired the brave volunteers. She traveled to Spain and, upon her return to the United States, wrote articles and made speeches on behalf of the Loyalist cause. To raise money for the Loyalists, she wrote a powerful documentary film called *The Spanish Earth*. A corporation was formed to finance the cost of the film. Calling themselves "Contemporary Historians," Dashiell Hammett, Lillian Hellman, Dorothy Parker, Herman Shumlin, poet Archibald MacLeish, and others contributed $500 each. The North American Committee for Spain, another organization sympathetic to the Loyalists, contributed $4,000. Writer Ernest Hemingway put up $2,750 and gave more later until the $13,000 needed to make the film was raised.

Ernest Hemingway (second from right) *in Spain during the filming of the documentary* The Spanish Earth

Lillian's screenplay for Dead End *was adapted from a Broadway play about life during the Great Depression.*

Narrated by Hemingway, *The Spanish Earth* played at movie theaters around the country. Ticket sales generated thousands of dollars to send equipment, medicine, and ambulances to the stricken war zone.

Soon afterward Hellman began work on her third screenplay, *Dead End*. This was adapted from a 1935 Broadway play of the same name by writer Sidney Kingsley. *Dead End* is a drama about children struggling to survive slum life during the Great Depression. It depicts the social problems that result from the rich and poor being crowded together in a big city. Starring Sylvia Sydney, Joel McCrea, and Humphrey Bogart, the film opened in New York in August 1937 and was highly praised by the critics. The day after *Dead End* opened, Lillian took off for Europe, spending a few weeks in Paris with friends before going on to Moscow to attend a theater festival.

The Spanish Earth *raised money for the Spanish Loyalists in their struggle against fascism.*

Both *The Spanish Earth* and *Dead End* reflected the social and political direction in which Lillian Hellman was moving. In the mid-1930s, she was sympathetic to the ideals that were part of Communist philosophy. With its promise of a classless society in which everything was shared equally by all people, Communism appeared (to some) to be a possible answer to the problems facing democratic countries.

Lillian visited Moscow during the time of Communist leader Joseph Stalin's purges. Stalin executed hundreds of thousands of Soviet citizens for treason and other alleged crimes against the state. He sent hundreds of thousands more to bleak prison camps near the Arctic Circle.

When Lillian returned to the United States, she claimed not to know of these atrocities. She had difficulty accepting the accusations against Stalin. She had always been impressed by the Soviet ideals of justice and equality. She later learned that Stalin had conducted the purges at the same time that he spoke in public about the heroic goals of Communism. Lillian eventually came to believe that her hosts limited her itinerary because they didn't want the American writer to know what was really happening.

Though disillusioned with the Soviet leadership, Lillian remained a supporter of the Soviet Union for many years. Her frequent involvement with liberal causes helped to fuel the rumor that she was a Communist Party member. Some people are convinced that she was a Communist Party member between 1938 and 1940, but the playwright herself never admitted this.

In 1938 Lillian plunged into work on her third play, *The Little Foxes*. Of all her plays, Lillian found *The Little Foxes* the most difficult to write. The play is set in the deep South of 1900. Lillian was a stickler for details. Everything about the time and setting needed to be authentic. With the help of a secretary and a researcher, the writer filled two notebooks, divided into sections covering American life and history from 1880 to 1900. The notebooks included studies of the cotton industry, the industrial South, the agricultural South, and black Southerners. There was also a historical background section covering the United States and Europe describing events such as the assassination of President McKinley and the 1904 Russo-Japanese War. Little of this material is mentioned specifically in the play, but appears in tiny details woven into the background and dialogue. This was how Lillian liked to work.

Writing *The Little Foxes* was also difficult because the play was partly based on Lillian's memories of her mother's family, most of whom she disliked. Like the Marxes and the

Newhouses, the Hubbard family in *The Little Foxes* is driven by greed and selfishness. Remembering childhood scenes in her grandmother's stuffy house, Lillian blended fact with fiction, creating a wealthy Southern clan obsessed with power. She revised and rewrote the play eight times but managed to complete the final script in less than a year.

In late May 1938, Dashiell Hammett suffered a nervous breakdown in Hollywood. When friends contacted Lillian, she arranged to have him flown to New York. She met him at the airport with an ambulance and took him to a hospital. She visited him daily until he was well enough to be discharged nearly a month later.

A publicity shot of the successful young playwright

As Hammett continued to improve, he took great interest in the development of Lillian's new play. Respectful of his tough criticism, Lillian found his sense and balance invaluable in the final shaping of *The Little Foxes*.

The Little Foxes is the story of the Hubbards, a family whose closeness is based on greed and power rather than love or affection. Regina Hubbard and her two brothers, Ben and Oscar, have an investment opportunity that they feel certain will make them rich. But Regina's husband, Horace, refuses to give Regina the money for her part of the deal. Ben and Oscar discover a way to steal the money from Horace and shut Regina out of their agreement. Regina, learning of the theft, subsequently blackmails her brothers to get back into the scheme. But when Horace learns of Regina's plan, he undermines her by deciding to ignore the theft and claim he loaned the money to the Hubbard brothers. At the play's climax, Regina murders her husband by deliberately refusing to give him his heart medication.

When the production was ready for casting, the choice of an actress to play the iron-willed Regina Hubbard became a problem. Several film stars turned down the part because they felt it would not show them in a favorable light. At this time, few actresses wanted roles that might depict them as aggressive women. The part was finally offered to Tallulah Bankhead, an intense young actress who read the script and accepted immediately. As the play went into rehearsal, Lillian had reservations about Bankhead because of her reputation for staging outrageous scenes. After a few rough starts and some rewrites, differences were worked out to everyone's satisfaction.

On February 2, 1939, *The Little Foxes* opened in New York. Once again, Lillian had created a tremendous success. The critics heaped praise on both the play and Tallulah

Tallulah Bankhead (left), *an actress known for her sometimes outrageous behavior, was perfect for the role of scheming, iron-willed Regina Hubbard in* The Little Foxes.

Bankhead's performance. *Life* magazine called *The Little Foxes* "the year's strongest play." The play ran for 410 performances before going on to tour the country. *The Little Foxes* also became an outstanding movie. Lillian wrote the script and Bette Davis starred as Regina Hubbard.

Weary but triumphant, Lillian decided to take time out from the pressures of her successful but hectic life. In June 1939, with money earned from *The Little Foxes*, she purchased Hardscrabble Farm, a sprawling 130-acre farm in Westchester County, New York. This was her first significant investment, and the first real house she had ever lived in. For the next 12 years, she and Hammett enjoyed Hardscrabble's tranquil privacy and peace. Surrounded by woods and a swampy lake, the main house had many rooms but managed to be comfortable and homey despite its size.

At Hardscrabble, Lillian raised pigs, lambs, and ducks. She planted asparagus and giant tomatoes, and made butter, cheese, and sausages. Sometimes she worked herself to weariness, but it was a good sort of tired—a change of pace from writing.

The farm offered an escape, yet Lillian enjoyed sharing it with friends who came to visit. Lillian loved to share the creole and Cajun food of her New Orleans childhood with visitors. Hammett, who had cut down on his drinking, spent most of his time at the farm. Their days together at Hardscrabble were among the most rewarding Lillian had known since they met.

Lillian's 1941 play Watch on the Rhine *tells the story of an innocent family drawn into the fight against fascism.*

SEVEN

Politics and Fame

1939–1946

"Somewhere there has to be what I want, too. Life goes too fast. I'd like to keep you with me, but I won't make you stay. Too many people used to make me do too many things. No, I won't make you stay."
—Regina Hubbard, *The Little Foxes*

In August 1939, to the confusion and distress of Soviet sympathizers, Joseph Stalin signed a non-aggression pact with Adolf Hitler. This meant that the Soviet Union and Nazi Germany would be allies. Soon after forming the pact, both nations invaded Poland, triggering the start of World War II. Early in 1940, the Soviet Union conquered Finland, and took over the territories of Latvia, Lithuania, and Estonia. Many Americans believed that Stalin's alliance with Hitler was proof that Communism was just another form of fascism. Lillian was deeply disturbed by the spread of fascism in Europe. She expressed her feelings in a play called *Watch on the Rhine*.

The play begins in the comfortable Washington, D.C. home of the Farrelly family. Their daughter, Sara, and her husband,

69

Kurt, have just returned from Europe where they have been active in the anti-Nazi underground resistance. A visiting German nobleman, Count Teck, is suspicious of Kurt Muller's sudden arrival. Snooping around, the curious count learns that Muller is about to return to Germany on a fake passport with a large amount of money he has collected to help victims of the Nazis.

Demanding to be paid off, Count Teck threatens Muller with exposure. Forced to kill Teck, Kurt Muller convinces his in-laws not to report the murder until he can leave the country. Suddenly, the Farrellys are accessories to a crime committed in the cause of anti-Nazism. Sara's mother, Fanny Farrelly, sums up the Farrellys' harsh awakening at the end of the play: "We've been shaken out of the magnolias," she declares.

Lillian read 25 books on European history as part of her research. The actual writing of the script took only eight months. She did most of the work at Hardscrabble Farm, spending long hours at the typewriter. Sometimes she barricaded herself in her study until early in the morning. When she finished the play in early 1941, she traveled to see Herman Shumlin at a hotel where he was staying. While she paced back and forth in the lobby, the producer sat in his room reading the play. At the end of the evening, he came downstairs to tell Lillian Hellman he was ready to put the new drama into production immediately.

The play opened on Broadway on April 1, 1941. It ran for 378 performances, receiving wide and popular acclaim. Lillian received her first New York Drama Critics Circle Award for *Watch on the Rhine*. One year later, the play was performed for President Franklin D. Roosevelt at the National Theater in Washington, D.C.

In December 1941, the Japanese—Germany's allies—
bombed the United States naval base in Pearl Harbor, Hawaii,
and the United States officially entered World War II. Lillian
and Dash worked at a number of projects to help the war
effort. To Lillian's dismay, Dash enlisted as a private in the
army despite the fact that he was 48 and in uncertain health.
But the army had raised the age limit for enlistment, and there
was nothing Lillian could do to stop him. Dash told Lillian that
the day he was accepted into the army was the happiest of
his life.

While Dash was in the service, Lillian wrote speeches for
politicians and delivered several of her own. At an authors'
luncheon on January 9, 1941, sponsored by the American
Bookseller's Association and the *New York Herald Tribune*,
she expressed her apprehension that the brutality and anti-
Semitism that characterized the Nazi regime might someday
come to menace the United States.

> I want to be able to go on saying that I am a Jew with-
> out being afraid of being called names or ending up in
> a prison camp or forbidden to walk down the street
> at night. Unless we are very careful and very smart
> and very protective of our liberties, a writer will be
> taking chances if he tells the truth, for as the lights
> dim out over Europe, they seem to flicker a little
> here, too.

In 1941 Hitler violated the non-aggression pact with Stalin
by invading the Soviet Union. Shocked by this betrayal, the
Soviet Union joined the Allies in the fight against Germany.
President Roosevelt felt it would be in the nation's interest to
promote a positive image of Russia. He asked Lillian Hellman
to help by writing a film for this purpose. Glad to oblige, the

North Star *was meant to show the courage of the Russian people as they fought against the Nazis.*

author joined forces with director William Wyler and producer Sam Goldwyn. Together they planned to develop a documentary that would show the bravery of the Russian people in the face of Nazi oppression.

Halfway through the project, William Wyler suddenly enlisted in the army. Another director, Lewis Milestone, was hired to replace him. Milestone, who had been born in Russia, and Lillian, who felt she knew a lot about Russia, did not get along. Milestone asked Lillian to make numerous changes in the script. Upset, Lillian complained to Sam Goldwyn. She was furious to learn he sided with Milestone. Lillian and Goldwyn had a fierce argument, and Lillian ended up buying her way out of the contract for $30,000. Upholding her convictions about writing meant more to her than the money or her eight-year association with Goldwyn.

When the picture *North Star* was finally released in November 1943, Lillian felt angry and frustrated. A musical score had been added to the story, and there were a lot of sleek Hollywood touches. She called it "a sentimental mess." Critics, however, praised the film's portrayal of Russian dignity.

In the summer of 1942, the ambitious playwright began work on still another play. *The Searching Wind* was similar to *Watch on the Rhine*. The new play also used Washington, D.C., in 1940 as its setting, but it included flashbacks to Rome in 1922, Berlin in 1923, and Paris in 1938. *The Searching Wind* gave Hellman more trouble than her previous plays. The play contained numerous time shifts and a large cast of characters.

The play opened on Broadway in April 1944. It had a run of 318 performances, but missed being awarded the Drama Critics' Circle Award by a single vote. Reviews were mixed. Some critics found it too rambling. Some believed that *The Searching Wind* was less successful than *Watch on the Rhine* because Dash, away in the army, was not around to give Lillian his usual advice.

In 1944 Lillian received an invitation from the Russian government to visit Moscow. She needed approval for the trip from the United States government. Travel during wartime was generally restricted, but President Roosevelt supported the playwright's journey as a cultural mission.

Lillian's trip to Russia was a harrowing experience. The first stage of the journey took her to Fairbanks, Alaska, where she was picked up by a Soviet flight crew. The war in Europe made it impossible to fly to the Soviet Union by the usual routes.

As a result, the primitive two-engine plane took 14 days to reach Moscow. During the flight, the single heater broke down. Because the plane's rudimentary flying instruments made it safe only to fly in good weather, the plane had to stop off in rickety way stations in the middle of the frozen Siberian wasteland whenever there was a storm.

Soon the shaken writer came down with a nasty case of pneumonia. She arrived in Moscow in November 1944, and spent time recovering at the American ambassador's residence. After her health improved, she joined in the social and cultural activities at Spasso House, the American embassy. One evening at an embassy dinner, Lillian met John Melby, a handsome

While visiting Moscow in 1944, Lillian met U.S. diplomat John Melby.

American foreign service officer. They discovered they had similar interests in the arts and world affairs.

Lillian saw a lot of John Melby, and the relationship soon turned into romance. Although Melby had a wife and two children in the United States, he fell deeply in love with Lillian and pressed her to make a commitment to him. The relationship was never to be more than an affair, however. As a foreign service officer, Melby was constantly assigned to various countries throughout the world. The couple continued to correspond with each other and stayed in touch for some time afterward.

Lillian stayed in Moscow for more than three months. She was extremely popular in Russia. Her interpreter, Raya Orlova, became a good friend. The two women maintained a warm relationship even after Lillian returned to America. In Moscow, the writer's hosts escorted her to Leningrad where she toured hospitals filled with wounded and dying soldiers. Here and on the streets of the city she was moved by the courage of the Russian people who had suffered greatly during the German invasion. Through Raya, her interpreter, Lillian got permission to visit the front lines of the war. Traveling by train was dangerous as well as uncomfortable during wartime. With limited water available on the train, the playwright had to wash her hands in snow and clean her teeth with cold tea. She ate mostly sardines and sausages.

Despite the hardships, Lillian received gracious treatment from Russians everywhere she went. Later she wrote about their extraordinary stamina and courtesy in an article in *Collier's*, an American magazine. Her most trying moments came during the inspection of the Maidanek concentration camp, abandoned by the Nazis as they fled Russia. After viewing the death ovens and open graves Lillian became physically ill.

Lillian visited the Maidanek concentration camp after it had been abandoned by the fleeing German army.

I was down in the blackness of deep water, pushed up to consciousness by monsters I could smell but not see, into a wildness of lions waiting to scrape my skin with their tongues, shoved down again, and up and down, covered with slime, pieces of me floating near my hands.

Not long after Hellman returned to the United States, World War II ended in Allied victory. By the summer of 1945, the writer's life returned to normal. After Hammett's discharge from the army, he divided his time between Hardscrabble Farm and an apartment in Manhattan. Though they had mutual friends and interests, it was important for Lillian and Dash to maintain their independence.

In 1946 Hellman began work on a new play, *Another Part of the Forest*. Although the play was the second in a planned trilogy about the Hubbard family portrayed in *The Little Foxes*, the playwright never wrote the third play. She felt the theme had been covered in the first two. She had done so much work for the background of *The Little Foxes* that additional research wasn't needed. While *The Little Foxes* concentrated on the Hubbards' obsession with power and money, *Another Part of the Forest* explored the psychological origin of these obsessions. To do this, Hellman moved the story back 20 years before the start of *The Little Foxes*.

Lillian did thorough research into every aspect of the periods and settings of her plays.

Patricia Neal played the young Regina in Another Part of the Forest, *Lillian's prequel to* The Little Foxes.

The playwright decided to direct *Another Part of the Forest* herself. She told friends she was tired of fighting with Herman Shumlin, the director and producer of her earlier plays, and she wanted to do her own thing. Needing someone to oversee the production, she hired Kermit Bloomgarden, a young man who had been Shumlin's general manager since 1935.

Lillian wanted to control her own work without any collaborators. Nevertheless, when it came to actually directing the actors, she knew very little about the technical aspects of the theater. Once, while directing a scene, she found herself at a loss as to how to tell the actor to move from the back of the stage to the front. Later Lillian admitted that she had fooled herself into thinking she was a director.

Another Part of the Forest opened in November 1946 and ran for 191 performances. Some critics liked the play, but others found it too melodramatic. Compared to Hellman's other successful plays, the run of this drama was among the shortest.

Lillian's father, Max, attended the opening of *Another Part of the Forest*, but behaved very strangely. He sat through the first act, crackling crisp dollar bills as he counted them aloud, annoying not only the theatergoers around him, but the actors on stage. At the end of Act I, the frail man stood up and loudly announced, "My daughter wrote this play. It gets better."

Lillian was later told by a doctor that her father was suffering from senile dementia, a form of mental illness. She postponed doing something about it for nearly six months. Finally, she was forced to commit Max Hellman to a hospital for the mentally ill in White Plains, not far from Hardscrabble Farm. Lillian visited her father as often as she could. Max Hellman died in 1948. Lillian felt that Max never forgave her for putting him in a mental hospital.

Lillian listens to a speech by Russian composer Dmitri Shostakovich at the Cultural and Scientific Conference for World Peace.

◀ EIGHT ▶

The Troubled Years

1947–1951

"Mine is often an irritable nature. If the groceries haven't arrived on time, or the corn grows stunted, or the phone rings too much, even with good news, I am as I have said, sometimes out of control. But when there is real trouble, the nervousness gets pushed down so far that calm can take its place, and although I pay high for disaster when it is long past, I am not sure that real trouble registers on me when it first appears."

—Lillian Hellman, *Scoundrel Time*

The fall of 1947 marked the start of a tense and troubling period for Lillian Hellman. J. Edgar Hoover, the director of the Federal Bureau of Investigation (FBI) charged that Communists were moving secretly into different industries in the United States, particularly the movie industry. Hoover and other government officials suspected that the Soviet Union wanted to force its form of government on the United States. Many Eastern European countries were being taken over by Communists. Putting a stop to the rise of Communism in the United States seemed urgent to some Americans. A congressional committee was formed called the House Un-American Activities Committee (HUAC). HUAC's purpose was to find Communists. Listening to the accusations made by Hoover, HUAC went all-out to target Hollywood. The members of the investigating committee maintained that the pro-Soviet films made during World War II were examples of Communists at work.

The FBI had been interested in Dashiell Hammett ever since his discharge from the army, partly because of his relationship with Lillian Hellman and partly because of his own affiliation with liberal causes. Sometimes FBI agents actually followed Dash. Lillian also continued to be active in liberal causes. In the late 1940s, her enthusiasm and support for Russia remained the same as it had been in the late 1930s.

In September 1947, HUAC held hearings in Washington to investigate Communist infiltration in the film industry. Congress had little trouble finding witnesses who would testify. Among the scores of witnesses ready to answer questions about their political beliefs and the surge of Communism in Hollywood were popular movie stars such as Gary Cooper, Robert Taylor, Adolphe Menjou, and Ronald Reagan, president of the Screen Actors' Guild.

On November 24, 1947, a group of Hollywood producers drafted a statement saying they would fire any writer or director in their employ who refused to answer questions asked by HUAC. Despite this harsh proclamation, one producer, two directors, and seven writers defied HUAC and would not answer the committee's questions. For their refusal to cooperate, the "Hollywood Ten" were cited for contempt of Congress, indicted by a grand jury, and sent to prison.

During this time, Lillian turned down an excellent movie contract because she was asked to sign a clause swearing that none of her political activities "would be different from what the studio would allow." Lillian refused to sign the contract. She didn't believe anyone should be able to control her activities or her beliefs. As a result, she was "blacklisted." She would never again be given an opportunity to write for the film indus-

FBI director J. Edgar Hoover (left) *believed that Communists were secretly infiltrating U.S. industries. Some popular movie stars, such as Ronald Reagan* (right), *were willing to testify about their political beliefs.*

try. The policy of blacklisting (denying employment to anyone who appeared politically unacceptable) became increasingly widespread. Many actors, writers, producers, and directors were blacklisted for refusing to compromise their beliefs. Practically anyone in Hollywood who had even a remote connection to a liberal cause was accused of subversive activity.

In response to the HUAC hearings and the blacklisting, Lillian wrote an angry article in the Screen Writers' Guild magazine.

> There has never been a single line or word of communism in any American picture at any time. There has never or seldom been ideas of any kind. Naturally men scared to make pictures about the American Negro, men who have only in the last year allowed the

word 'Jew' to be spoken in a picture, men who took
more than ten years to make an anti-Fascist picture,
these are frightened men, and you pick frightened men
to frighten first. Judas goats: they'll lead the others,
maybe to the slaughter for you. ... They frighten mighty
easy and they talk mighty bad. For one week they made
us, of course, the laughingstock of the educated and
decent world. I suggest the rest of us don't frighten
so easy. It's still not un-American to fight the enemies
of one's country. Let's fight.

Lillian spoke out against blacklisting and the HUAC hearings.

Henry Wallace

Unfortunately, Hollywood remained paralyzed by fear and suspicion, and the playwright's impassioned plea evoked little response. Nevertheless, Lillian continued her political activity. In 1948, when former vice president Henry Wallace ran for the presidency on the Progressive Party ticket, Lillian joined his campaign, becoming one of his most active supporters. She headed a committee called Women for Wallace. The committee developed a party platform that urged greater cooperation with the Soviet Union, a reduction in weapons, and an end to the military draft.

During the campaign, Wallace faced accusations that he was under Communist control. Though several Communist Party members did belong to the Progressive Party, Lillian countered the accusations by promising that if the campaign was Communist-controlled, she would resign. In a speech she gave in February 1948 at a Women for Wallace luncheon, Lillian continued to deny the presence of Communists in the Wallace movement. Her efforts, however, were unsuccessful. Damaged by the allegations, Wallace was soon out of the running.

In 1948 Lillian accepted an assignment from the *New York Star* newspaper to go to Yugoslavia, where she interviewed Yugoslav leader Marshal Tito. Tito had just attracted the world's attention by being the first Communist leader to break with the Soviet Union. Once again, Lillian found herself in a foreign country as it experienced a major political crisis. She wrote of her experiences in a series of six articles for the Star.

In 1948 Lillian interviewed Marshal Tito, Communist leader of Yugoslavia.

In the first months of 1949, the American public continued to grow alarmed about the Communist threat. Many people began to believe that Communism was more than a political system. They were concerned that it might be a conspiracy to destroy the democratic way of life in America.

To promote the idea of peaceful coexistence with the Soviet Union, Hellman joined a number of prominent writers and artists in hosting the Cultural and Scientific Conference for World Peace. Among the participants were scientist Albert Einstein, composer Leonard Bernstein, and architect Frank Lloyd Wright. Because the gathering was held at the Waldorf Astoria Hotel in New York City, it came to be known as the Waldorf Conference.

On March 25, 1949, the opening of the Waldorf Conference turned into a major public demonstration. Picketers surrounded the hotel waving signs denouncing Stalin. A few groups sang "The Star Spangled Banner." Others knelt in prayer. Inside the Waldorf ballroom, 2,000 people listened while magazine editor Norman Cousins attacked the Communist party. Cousins was one of the few anti-Soviets invited to the meeting.

"I ask you to believe," said Cousins, "that this group is without standing and without honor in its own country." He also said the conference represented "a small political group which owes its allegiance not to America but to an outside government." When Cousins finished, Lillian walked up to the microphone. With quiet composure, the playwright responded to the man who had just stepped down from the platform.

"I would recommend, Mr. Cousins, that when you are invited out to dinner, you wait until you get home before you talk about your hosts."

The crowd responded with loud laughter and applause. *Life* magazine published a photo of Lillian with the caption, "Mastermind." There was no question that the playwright had been very much in charge at the conference.

While in Europe the year before, Lillian had met the Spanish playwright Emmanuel Roblès and decided to do an adaptation of his play *Montserrat*. In the fall of 1949, *Montserrat* opened on Broadway. Earlier that same month, a production of *Another Part of the Forest* opened in Moscow under the title *Ladies and Gentlemen*. A few days later, an operatic version of *The Little Foxes* called *Regina*, written by Marc Blitzstein, also made its debut.

While the Moscow production received praise, *Montserrat* fared less well in New York. Set in South America during the 19th century, the play explores whether or not individual lives can be sacrificed justly to advance a revolution that might benefit millions of people. As far as critical and financial success were concerned, Lillian had done better.

Lillian's next original play was called *The Autumn Garden*. The play focuses on how a group of middle-aged characters makes and breaks their faith in each other.

Dash was again on hand to help with the play. Although he was experiencing a case of writer's block that would become permanent, he continued to influence Lillian's work. When he read the first draft of the new play, he told Lillian, "It's worse than bad, it's half-good."

She was so humiliated that she tore up the manuscript and decided to try again. There was one speech in particular she kept working and reworking but just couldn't get right. Finally, exhausted, she went upstairs to bed. In the morning she came downstairs to discover that sometime during the night, Dash

Fredric March in
The Autumn Garden

had written the speech for her. He had succeeded in saying exactly what she had in mind. On March 7, 1951, *The Autumn Garden* opened in New York to mixed reviews. Lillian felt it was her best play, but not all the critics agreed. The production closed after only 102 performances.

Lillian was disappointed, but she continued to receive honors as a playwright. She traveled to the University of Michigan where she read student dramas for the prestigious Hopewood Awards. For years, winners of the Hopewood Awards had gone on to become important writers. Traditionally, noted authors were invited to judge the annual competition.

Despite her disappointment in *The Autumn Garden*, Lillian reached middle age in relative tranquility. She tried to busy herself around Hardscrabble Farm, working in the garden and leading a peaceful life with Dash.

Senator Joseph McCarthy's accusations that the U.S. government had been infiltrated by Communists began a terribly devastating era in American politics.

NINE

The McCarthy Crisis

1950–1958

"I believed that I am telling the truth, not the survivors' consolation, when I say that the disasters of the McCarthy period were, in many ways, good for me: I learned things, I got rid of much I didn't need. But I am angrier now than I hope I will ever be again; more disturbed now than when it all took place."
—Lillian Hellman, *Three*

In 1950 Joseph McCarthy, a little-known Republican senator from Wisconsin, delivered a speech in Wheeling, West Virginia. In a ringing voice, he claimed proof that the government of the United States had been infiltrated by Communists. He added that not only did he know who these traitors were, but that he had a list of their names in his hand.

With this dramatic announcement, Senator McCarthy ushered in one of the most destructive periods in American politics. During the McCarthy era, Congress held numerous hearings in which people testified about their own political activities, as well as those of other people. Some, who refused to answer questions, were arrested for contempt and jailed.

Those who chose to plead the Fifth Amendment—meaning they refused to answer on the grounds they might incriminate themselves (make themselves look guilty)—usually faced career setbacks and social ostracism. Under a law called the Smith Act, admitted Communists could also be prosecuted and sent to jail for advocating the overthrow of the U.S. government.

While Dashiell Hammett had always been ready to lend his name or contribute money to radical causes, his political activity never really amounted to much. Despite this, in the spring of 1951, three FBI agents paid a visit to Hardscrabble Farm. They did not produce a search warrant, but Dash and Lillian invited them in anyway. Trying to appear calm, Lillian drove them around the estate's 130 acres. She suspected why the agents were there. Shortly before the FBI visit, Dash had become one of the trustees of an organization that posted bail for people being prosecuted under the Smith Act. When some American Communists were convicted, their supporters set up a bail fund for them. In June 1951, four of the men jumped bail and fled. The FBI agents came to Hardscrabble because they suspected that Communists were hiding out there.

When the missing men were not found, Dash received a summons to appear in court for questioning. At his court appearance on July 9, 1951, Dash pleaded the Fifth Amendment, refusing to answer all questions because he felt the court had no right to invade his privacy. Dash was ruled in contempt of court. In a state of panic and confusion, Lillian raced around New York trying to raise money for bail, which she expected to be about $100,000. She pawned all her jewelry but only got $17,000 for it. She also approached several friends, who contributed checks, but the total collected was still far from the sum she thought she needed. In tears, Hellman returned to court to learn that the judge had denied Dash bail. He had been sentenced to six months in prison. That was bad enough news, but there was an additional blow. Far behind in payments of income taxes, Dash also owed more than $100,000 to the Internal Revenue Service (IRS). For the rest of his life, all his earnings would go directly to the government to pay this debt.

Lillian did her best to help Dash, but she was having financial problems of her own. While she had earned a lot of money writing, she had also been very extravagant. For the past two decades, she had spent large sums traveling, entertaining, and buying expensive clothes, with no thought of saving. The only investment she had made was the farm. Her recent plays had not done well, and since she was blacklisted by Hollywood, there was no movie work. And the IRS had discovered that Lillian also owed back taxes. Now Lillian had to face reality.

Dashiell Hammett being taken to jail in 1951

When the IRS found that she owed back taxes, Lillian (shown here in her Manhattan home) had to give up some of the luxuries she had grown accustomed to.

In order to meet her overwhelming expenses, there was only one thing left to do. She sold Hardscrabble, the refuge that she and Dash had grown to love.

After Dash went to prison, he sent Lillian a note through his attorney, telling her to take one of the trips to Europe she loved so much. He assured her it was not necessary for Lillian to prove that she loved him after all their years together. Lillian realized he did not want her to see him in prison. She did what he asked. She took a short trip to Europe, but when she came back, it was time to face her own ordeal. On February 21, 1952, the playwright received a subpoena to appear before the House Committee on Un-American Activities. While she had never been cowardly about her political beliefs, Lillian could not help but feel terrified of the anti-Communist frenzy that was sweeping the country.

Lillian was determined not to say anything in court that might be damaging to others, but Dash urged her not to be a martyr. Released from prison in January, he told her she was not the kind of person who could survive prison. Having come out of prison in poor health, he knew only too well.

A young Washington lawyer named Joseph Rauh agreed to represent Lillian. On her first visit to his office, she told him there were three things she would not do: plead the Fifth Amendment, name names, or go to jail.

Rauh was confident about defending Lillian because he believed she had never been a Communist. But he felt it would be best to come up with some kind of compromise. He wrote a letter for Lillian to send to HUAC. She didn't like his wording and rewrote it. Two days before her scheduled appearance, HUAC received the letter, in which the playwright asserted her innocence of all politically subversive activities and beliefs.

> I am not willing, now or in the future, to bring bad trouble to people, who in my past association with them were completely innocent of any talk or any action that was disloyal. To hurt innocent people whom I knew many years ago in order to save myself is, to me, inhuman and indecent and dishonorable. I cannot and will not cut my conscience to fit this year's fashions.

Lillian concluded the letter by repeating her desire to cooperate with HUAC, providing she could confine her comments

Between Dashiell Hammett's imprisonment and her own HUAC ordeal, 1952 was a troubling year for Lillian.

to her personal beliefs and activities and not those of other people. She also said if she were pressured to tell about the activities of others, she would be forced to take the Fifth Amendment.

But HUAC rejected her offer to testify only about herself. The committee announced that it would not permit witnesses to make the rules under which they testified. For the next few days, Lillian was understandably tense and nervous. She tried to put HUAC out of her mind by shopping or going to the zoo. She even bought herself an expensive designer dress she couldn't really afford. Lillian liked to be well-dressed for public appearances of every kind. On May 21, 1952, she was called to appear before a HUAC subcommittee.

It took a lot of courage to climb up the steep flight of steps to the building in Washington, D.C. where the hearings were held. When Lillian entered the front hall called the rotunda, she saw a crowd of people waiting for the elevators. Holding on to the brass handrail, she walked up the marble circular staircase. As she entered the Caucus room, Joe Rauh came to meet her. He smiled at her, but she found it difficult to smile back. Dozens of photographers' flash bulbs went off in Lillian's face. Between flashes, the startled writer saw 20 or 30 reporters sitting along one wall. Row after row of seats were filled with people staring straight at her. Joe Rauh held Lillian's elbow, steering her to a table 20 feet from a platform that looked like a stage. A moment later the HUAC commit-

The HUAC hearings, instigated by McCarthy (right), *destroyed the lives of many innocent people.*

tee filed in and sat at a table on the platform. The vast room grew still. Lillian heard her name called. Clenching a handkerchief in her left hand, she stood to be sworn in.

At first the committee's questions seemed routine. Lillian gave her name, place of birth, and occupation. There was a slight pause. Then the committee stated the allegation that she, Lillian Hellman, was a Communist Party member and asked her to respond to the charge. She declined to answer on the grounds that she might incriminate herself. Despite her resolve not to, Lillian had taken the Fifth Amendment.

With great earnestness, Lillian referred the committee to the letter they had received from her two days earlier. She asked them to consider very seriously what she had written. Committee Counsel Frank Tanner asked Lillian if she expected the committee not to ask her any questions regarding the activities of others in the Communist Party. Lillian replied that she didn't think that was what her letter stated.

Now everyone on the committee wanted to read her letter. Hellman's attorney quickly passed around the copies he had prepared. He made sure that members of the press also got copies. At this point, a committee member asked that Hellman's letter be entered into the record. Because the letter seemed to imply that Lillian was pleading the Fifth Amendment to protect others and not herself, many people saw her as a heroine—motivated by loyalty rather than self-protection.

Lillian's questioning by HUAC took one hour and seven minutes. She was neither found in contempt nor sent to prison. The playwright had managed to accomplish what others had not.

A few weeks after her HUAC appearance, Lillian planned to appear at the Kaufman Auditorium in Manhattan to narrate the concert version of *Regina*. Uncertain as to how the public would react, she hesitated to show up, but was finally persuaded. Wearing the same designer dress she had worn at the hearing, Hellman walked slowly on to the stage. Immediately the entire audience rose to its feet in a rousing ovation. It was an exciting victory for Lillian Hellman.

Unfortunately, Lillian's problems were far from over. A few months after her HUAC appearance, she found herself desperately in need of money. She needed a surefire hit to help her with finances. She thought that perhaps a revival of her first play, *The Children's Hour*, could be that hit. Undaunted by her earlier difficulties in dealing with actors, she decided to direct the revival herself. Though Lillian was blacklisted by Hollywood, she still had friends on Broadway. Reviving this drama seemed particularly appropriate, since it was about how lives could be wrecked by suspicion—just as had happened to so many during the McCarthy catastrophe.

The revival of *The Children's Hour* opened in December 1952 to an enthusiastic reception. It ran for 189 performances, providing the playwright with some much-needed income, but she still continued to look for work. The IRS had reviewed her tax returns and determined that she owed still more money.

In 1953 Lillian traveled to Italy to write a screenplay for director Alexander Korda. She received much less for this work than she had ever earned for similar writing. Having been one of the highest paid screenwriters in Hollywood, Lillian was understandably upset. Back in the United States, she edited a collection of letters by the 19th-century Russian playwright Anton Chekov.

She decided next to adapt *L'Alouette (The Lark)*, a French drama about Joan of Arc. Though the story took place at a very different time in history, Lillian found many similarities between the story and her own experience. *The Lark* was about a woman coerced by the government to testify against her own beliefs. After finding two college students who could translate the play, Hellman began writing the adaptation. Soon, however, Lillian's work was interrupted.

In the summer of 1955, Dashiell Hammett suffered a heart attack. Although he recovered partially, he was mostly bed-ridden and dependent on Lillian for the next four years. She purchased a house on Martha's Vineyard, an island off the southeast corner of Massachusetts. Though Dash could not stay in the Vineyard house all year-round because of the cold winters, he enjoyed frequent vacations in the octagon-shaped guest house.

Lillian devoted much of her time to caring for her ailing companion, but she still managed to complete her adaptation of *The Lark*. With actress Julie Harris as Joan of Arc, the play

Lillian's adaptation of a French drama, The Lark, *starred Julie Harris* (left) *and Boris Karloff.*

Lillian collaborated with composer Leonard Bernstein (center) *and director Tyrone Guthrie* (right) *on the musical* Candide.

opened in November 1955 and was both a critical and financial success. *The New York Daily News* and *The New York Times* printed very favorable reviews.

For the next three years, Lillian worked on only one project. *Candide* was a collaborative effort between Lillian, composer Leonard Bernstein, director Tyrone Guthrie, and poet Richard Wilbur. The mix of talents did not blend well. Lillian often found it difficult to be a good team player. The final outcome was unsuccessful, and *Candide* closed after 73 performances. Frustrated by this failure, Lillian searched once again for a fresh theme and memorable characters.

Julian encourages his suspicious sisters to enjoy his success in Toys in the Attic, *Lillian's 1960 drama.*

◀ TEN ▶

Toys in the Attic
1958–1961

"I would say I wanted to get everything straight for the days after his death when I would write his biography and he would say that I was not to bother writing his biography because it would turn out to be the history of Lillian Hellman with an occasional reference to a friend called Hammett."
—Lillian Hellman, *An Unfinished Woman*

On occasion some writers experience a miserable emptiness known as writer's block. Lillian Hellman was no exception. When it happened this time, she felt it was brought on by her frustration with *Candide* and her concern for Dash. As he had so often before, Dash came to the rescue by spurring Lillian on with a new idea.

He told her a story about a man who believes other people when say they love him and want him to be rich. The man becomes rich and finds out that the same people really don't like him that way. He messes things up and ends very badly.

Lillian thought about this. She was not sure where the story had originated, but that didn't matter. She worked with the idea until it became *Toys in the Attic*.

Set in 1912 New Orleans, *Toys in the Attic* is more auto-biographical than Lillian's other plays. It tells the story of two unmarried sisters, Carrie and Anna, who build their lives around their younger brother, Julian. The two women—who resemble Hellman's aunts, Jenny and Hannah—want Julian to be rich and successful. So far he has been a failure at everything he has tried. The similarity of Julian to Max Hellman, though exaggerated, is apparent.

When Julian suddenly shows up at his sisters' home with a young new wife, bearing money and gifts, his sisters no longer have a purpose in life. It comes as a shock that Julian is no longer their "toy." Though with Julian's money they will be able to lead independent lives, they still want to hold on to their brother. Their wish is granted when Lily, Julian's wife, deliberately ruins a business deal for her husband in the mistaken belief he is interested in another woman. Once again weak and penniless, Julian is forced to lean on his sisters. Because of his dependence, the family is reunited, held fast by the suffocating bonds with which they started.

Opening on February 25, 1960, *Toys in the Attic* ran for 556 performances and was greeted with wide acclaim. In May 1960, the writer won her second Drama Critics Circle Award.

This should have been one of the happiest times in Lillian's life, but her preoccupation with Dash's illness had become a painful priority. Suffering from lung cancer and emphysema, Dash dragged himself to rehearsals of *Toys in the Attic*. Soon, however, he was unable to leave his bed. When he announced that he was going to put himself into a nursing home, Lillian panicked. Appealing to his vanity, she convinced him how much she needed him. Converting her large, sunny workroom and living room into living quarters, she tried to make Dash as comfortable as possible.

The last year of Dashiell Hammett's life was sad and agonizing. Aware that he didn't have much time, he refused to see old friends and clung to Lillian like a child. The emphysema grew so bad that breathing became exhausting. He grew increasingly weak. Lillian made a habit of setting her alarm clock every two hours, all night. She would sit with him until the attack slackened a little and he could rest between spasms. Eventually, the situation grew so serious that Dash had to be moved to a hospital. Nine days later, on January 10, 1961, Dashiell Hammett died.

Three hundred people attended Dashiell Hammett's funeral. Lillian, his companion of 30 years, realized he would probably not want any words spoken about him, but she spoke anyway. She said he didn't always think very well of the society he lived in, yet when it punished him he made no complaints. She called him a man of honor and bravery.

On January 13, 1961, Dashiell Hammett was buried in Arlington National Cemetery.

Dashiell Hammett is buried in Arlington National Cemetery.

Lillian at age 62

◀ ELEVEN ▶

Another Career

1961–1976

"But I am not yet old enough to like the past better than the present, although there are nights when I have a passing sadness for the unnecessary pains, the self-made foolishness that was, is and will be."
—Lillian Hellman, *An Unfinished Woman*

Outwardly, Lillian appeared to be coping well with Dashiell Hammett's death. In the spring of 1961, she accepted an invitation to present a series of lectures about writing at Harvard University. Though she personally doubted that writing was a skill that could be taught, she found teaching a challenge. As a teacher, she was alternately strict and maternal, sometimes bringing refreshments for her students and chatting with them after class. Though Lillian made it quite clear that she would teach the course her way, she was popular with many students. After her teaching stint ended, she admitted that the students were much better educated and poised than when she was a student at NYU.

Over the next few years, Lillian received several distinguished honors. Brandeis University awarded her its Theater Arts Medal, Yeshiva University presented her with an Achievement Award, and Wheaton College conferred an honorary doctorate. She was also elected to the honorary position of vice president of the National Institute of Arts and Letters.

While all these tributes were flattering, Lillian wanted to keep writing. During her stay at Harvard, she happened to read a novel about Jewish family life called *How Much* that triggered an idea for another play—*My Mother, My Father, and Me*.

The story reminded her of her own family, but instead of writing a serious drama as she always had, she attempted to

Ruth Gordon (right) *starred in the unsuccessful comedy* My Mother, My Father, and Me. *Gower Champion* (left) *directed the play.*

Lillian received honors from many colleges and universities. Here, she accepts an honorary degree from Smith College.

make *My Mother, My Father, and Me* into a comedy. Unfortunately, light treatments were not her area of expertise. On March 21, 1963, the play opened on Broadway. It was a flop. Reviews were poor, and the production closed after only 17 performances. After this failure, Lillian never again tried to write for the stage. She wanted to write books and finally be independent of producers and directors.

———○———

Even after Lillian's bitter encounter with HUAC, she was not discouraged from political involvement. In 1963 she became inspired by the civil rights movement. On an assignment for the *Ladies Home Journal*, she went to Washington, D.C., to cover the famous civil rights march led by Dr. Martin Luther King, Jr.

Lillian wrote about the 1963 civil rights march on Washington, D.C., for Ladies Home Journal.

By 1965 Hellman had grown increasingly disillusioned with the repressive government of the Soviet Union. She joined a group of American writers in signing an open letter to the Russian premier asking leniency for two Soviet authors who were on trial for publishing books outside the Soviet Union. In 1966 Lillian traveled to Russia, her first trip there in 22 years. Among the good friends she still had there was her translator, Raya. Lillian's plays were still popular with Russian theater audiences.

On another trip to Russia in 1967, the playwright was asked to address a Writer's Congress in Moscow. Assuming that she would be able to say anything she wanted, Hellman accepted the invitation. She waited, speech in hand, in the great hall where the delegates were meeting.

At first she refused to let anyone review her notes, but when she was told she would not be permitted to speak unless a copy was submitted, she reluctantly agreed. Much to her shock and disbelief, her turn to speak was passed over without explanation. She returned to her hotel, telephoned the *New York Times*, gave them the speech, packed her bags, and caught a morning plane to Paris. Lillian finally understood firsthand what the Soviet Union thought of free speech.

On her return to the United States, Lillian became involved in a variety of projects. One of them was teaching a freshman seminar in writing at Yale University. On the first day of class, she announced to her students that she was teaching an "exploratory" course. She told them the class would work only if they talked openly to one another. Interruption and argument were an acceptable part of class discussion. Lillian made it clear that she would not be instructing them in grammar or composition, but she would be there to help with suggestions that they were free to accept or reject.

She showed her students how to go through a manuscript and eliminate unnecessary words. Simple words were substituted for flowery ones. She pointed out that strong story lines and characters were essential to good writing. Sometime during the course, Lillian confided to her class that she was thinking of writing her memoirs, and that they would not look like a book of memoirs by anybody else.

But before she began writing about herself, Hellman finished editing a collection of Hammett's writings called *The Big Knockover: Stories and Short Novels by Dashiell Hammett*. Though Dash had stopped writing years before his death, Lillian wanted to honor the most important person in her adult life.

In 1969 Lillian wrote a memoir called *An Unfinished Woman*. A completely new career opened up for the writer. The style of this book was far different from the chronological style of most autobiographies. Hellman dipped into her memories, writing about people and events in no particular order. Some critics said that *An Unfinished Woman* resembled a series of literary sketches rather than an autobiography, but the public loved the book despite its form, or maybe because of it.

In 1970 the book became a bestseller and won a National Book Award for Arts and Letters. The self-portrait that emerged from the pages of *An Unfinished Woman* was one that fascinated critics and readers alike. The name Lillian Hellman had been associated mostly with the theater. Now readers around the country learned about the New Orleans boardinghouse, Sophronia, Lillian's aunts, her life in Hollywood, Hardscrabble Farm, her visit to the Russian front lines, and of course, Dash. Dash's presence was everywhere in *An Unfinished Woman*. While Hellman never wrote a complete biography of the mystery writer, she still managed to evoke a vivid image of her companion.

In the early 1970s, Hellman's political interest veered in new directions. Lillian was alarmed by moves made by the FBI and the CIA to silence those who protested civil rights abuses and the Vietnam War. She formed the Committee for Public Justice—a watchdog organization of people who monitored government activities. Calling on prominent writers, such as John Hersey and William Styron, and director Mike Nichols, the committee soon had more than 100 members. One of the recruited members, cartoonist Jules Feiffer, called Lillian the organization's prime motivator.

Lillian won a National Book Award in 1970 for her memoir An Unfinished Woman.

> She got on the phone and brought together a group of lawyers and professors and writers and statesmen and a millionaire or two and formed the Committee. She chaired the meetings, helped raise the funds, got others to raise more funds, thrashed out agendas, and set up a series of well-covered meetings across the country. No other writer I know would know how to do this.

From 1970 through 1982, Hellman continued to be the central figure of the committee. She raised money through benefit dinners and started a newsletter called *Justice Department Watch*. The publication issued reports about government violations of civil liberties, winning support for the committee's activities.

Lillian never ceased her support of liberal causes. Here she attends a fundraiser for presidential candidate Eugene McCarthy.

Busy as she was, Lillian found enough time and energy to work on yet another book of memoirs. This second volume was called *Pentimento*. Published in 1973, *Pentimento* was even more successful than *An Unfinished Woman*. Attracted by her first bestseller, readers were eager to read more. Lillian did not disappoint them. In a brief introduction she explained the meaning of the title.

> Old paint on canvas, as it ages, sometimes becomes transparent. When that happens it is possible in some pictures to see the original lines: a tree will show through a woman's dress, a child makes way for a dog, a large boat is no longer on an open sea. This is called pentimento because the painter 'repented'—changed his mind. Perhaps it would be as well to say that the old conception, replaced by a later choice, is a way of seeing and then seeing again. That is all I mean about the people in this book. The paint has aged now and

> I wanted to see what was there for me once, what is
> there for me now.

Pentimento is another journey back in time, told in vig-
nettes. The most famous of these stories is "Julia," about
Lillian's childhood friend. Julia, a wealthy young heiress, studied
medicine in Vienna prior to World War II. After joining the
Austrian anti-fascist underground, the young woman was cap-
tured and killed by the Nazis in 1937. Before her capture, she
managed to contact her friend Lillian and asked her to smug-
gle $50,000 in cash from Paris to Berlin. The money was to
be used to help resistance fighters escape the Nazis.

Lillian and Julia meet briefly between trains in a restaurant.
Lillian gives Julia a hat with the money stuffed in the lining.
Shortly after this encounter, Lillian receives a wire informing
her of Julia's death. She flies to London, brings Julia's knife-
slashed body home to New York, and has the body cremated.

The revelation of these gripping episodes in Lillian's life
added to her image as a bold and daring woman. A number
of critics, however, believed that Lillian made up Julia, basing
her on a woman named Muriel Buttinger, whose life was
remarkably like Julia's.

In 1976 the last book in Lillian's trilogy of memoirs, *Scoundrel Time*, made its debut. *Scoundrel Time* was on the bestseller list for 23 weeks. The book was different from the first
two memoirs, concentrating on the McCarthy era and Lillian's
encounter with HUAC. Lillian attacked anti-Communist liberals
who did not come to the defense of those being persecuted,
presenting herself as a lone fighter against political harassment.
Some critics found Lillian's version distorted, arguing that many
anti-Communist liberals did oppose McCarthyism. Despite
criticism, *Scoundrel Time* received highly favorable reviews.

Movie star Elizabeth Taylor (right) *made her Broadway debut as Regina Hubbard in a 1981 revival of one of Lillian's most successful plays,* The Little Foxes.

TWELVE

Journey's End

1976–1984

"I have written here that I have recovered. I mean it only in a worldly sense because I do not believe in recovery. The past, with its pleasures, its rewards, its foolishness, its punishments, is there for each of us forever, and it should be."
—Lillian Hellman, *Scoundrel Time*

In May 1976, Lillian Hellman was awarded an honorary degree as an "illustrious woman of letters" by Columbia University. She also delivered the commencement address at Mt. Holyoke College and was awarded the prestigious MacDowell Medal for her contribution to literature. In March 1977, still another tribute was given the writer when she appeared as a presenter at the Academy Awards ceremony in Hollywood. Jane Fonda, the actress who played Lillian in the film version of *Julia* that was soon to be released, introduced the 72-year-old author in an impassioned speech, listing her accomplishments and praising her bravery despite political oppression. Walking slowly because of her arthritis, the frail woman in the dark evening dress moved forward. Heavy glasses almost covered her deeply wrinkled face. As she approached the podium, the audience rose to its feet in a prolonged standing ovation.

Jane Fonda played Lillian Hellman and Jason Robards played Dashiell Hammett in the 1977 film Julia, *based on a chapter of Lillian's memoir* Pentimento.

Not everyone was ready to honor Lillian Hellman. Eric Sevareid, a popular news commentator, denounced Hellman on the CBS Evening News the following night. He said he considered it "shameful that playwright Lillian Hellman accepted applause, not for her art, but for her political activities in the McCarthy era."

Julia opened amid widespread publicity at theaters across the country in October 1977. In the film, actress Vanessa Redgrave played the title role of Julia and Jane Fonda played Lillian Hellman. Some reviewers criticized the over-glorification of Lillian's character, but the movie was a box office success.

Over the next few years, Lillian's reputation was attacked from various quarters. On January 25, 1980, talk-show host Dick Cavett invited novelist and critic Mary McCarthy (no relation to the senator) to discuss overrated writers. McCarthy's response was to jump on Lillian Hellman, calling her a bad and dishonest writer. When Cavett asked her to explain this statement, McCarthy charged that everything Hellman ever wrote was a lie. A few days later Cavett received a call from an angry and upset Hellman. She felt that the host should have defended her. Cavett apologized and invited Hellman to appear on one of his programs to respond to McCarthy's remarks. Lillian refused, saying she would look foolish going on national television to claim she was not a liar. A week later she brought a $2.25 million lawsuit against McCarthy, Cavett, and the Public

Writer Mary McCarthy accused Lillian of fabricating much of her memoirs.

Broadcasting Corporation, charging them with insulting her character and reputation.

The lawsuit dragged on for several years. Some people thought that Mary McCarthy had gone too far. Others questioned whether it was right for Lillian to sue. Author Norman Mailer wrote a public appeal asking both women to end the suit. He felt that for the two writers to attack each other this way was bad for all writers. Hellman pressed McCarthy for a public apology, but the novelist flatly refused, saying she was entitled to her opinion. She further indicated that she had evidence that parts of "Julia" were not only exaggerated but untrue. Whether Lillian crossed the line between fact and fiction was never proven. The case never made it to trial.

In 1980, though suffering from failing eyesight and lung problems, Hellman wrote a short autobiographical novella called *Maybe*, the story of an imaginary friend named Sarah. Lillian wrote the book as a series of flashbacks, in which Sarah tells lies and constantly denies the truth. Several critics thought Hellman might have been offering an explanation for her own distortion of truth, a kind of "maybe" about "Julia" and her other memoirs. *Maybe* was the last piece of writing the author did by herself.

In 1981 Hellman suffered a heart attack and had to have a pacemaker installed. After the surgery, she felt unable to live alone and went to stay at the Beverly Hills home of her friends William and Talli Wyler. With plenty of rooms, the Wylers found it easy to accommodate their friend. Lillian brought along a nurse and cook who had been with her for many years.

Living in separate quarters, Lillian installed her own phone and maintained her privacy. When she found it difficult to climb the flight of stairs that led to her part of the house, she hired a UCLA college student to carry her up and down and also to drive her car. Though her health was failing, her spirit did not deteriorate.

In her own way, Lillian continued to write, working on *Eating Together: Recollections and Recipes* with her friend Peter Feibleman. The slim cookbook included accounts of places and the meals associated with them. Some of the recipes were New Orleans-based. Others were from San Francisco, New York, Boston, Palm Beach, Maine, Mexico, Paris, London, Rome, and Cairo. Much of the time, Lillian worked by dictating into a machine as she lay propped up on pillows in bed. None of her contributions were over three pages, since she had only enough breath for short periods of dictation.

During the summer of 1984, though her health continued to fail, Lillian insisted on going fishing with her friend Jack Koontz. Fishing had always been one of her favorite activities. Now she could barely hold her fishing rod steady, but with Jack's help, she soon caught a fairly big fish. He held it up close to her so she could feel how big it was. The week before she died, Lillian called Koontz, asking him to arrange their next fishing expedition.

Persistently keeping her social engagements to the very end, Hellman was carried to the house of a friend for dinner one summer evening. The next day, June 30, 1984, the feisty playwright died of heart failure at the age of 79.

Lillian Hellman was buried under a tall pine tree in Abel's Hill Cemetery in Chilmark, Massachusetts, on her beloved Martha's Vineyard. People from all over the country came to attend the funeral. Celebrities from New York, Hollywood, and elsewhere arrived in large numbers, some to deliver special eulogies. One of the most touching was that of Hellman's friend, writer John Hersey.

I'd like to say a few words about Lillian's anger. Most of us were startled by it from time to time. Anger was her essence. It was at the center of that passionate temperament. It informed her art. The little foxes snapped at each other, we could see their back hairs bristle, we could smell their foxiness—they were real and alive because of the current of anger that ran through them, as it did through so many of Lillian's characters. What I want to say is that this voltage of Lillian's was immensely important and valuable to our time. It electrified a mood of protest. The protest was that of every great writer. Life ought to be better than this.... Dear Lillian, you are a finished woman now. I mean 'finished' in its better sense. You shone with a high finish of integrity, decency, and uprightness. You have given us this anger to remember and use in a bad world. We thank you, we honor you, and we all say good-bye to you now with a love that should claim that anger of yours forever.

Lillian's will directed that the bulk of her nearly $4 million estate, earned from the success of her plays and memoirs, be placed in two separate trust funds. One was the Lillian Hellman Fund, whose purpose was to award gifts and grants to selected applicants in the arts and sciences. The other was the Dashiell Hammett Fund, which served the same purpose but stipulated that the applicant's goals be consistent with Hammett's political and social beliefs. Lillian also left money to close friends such as Peter Feibleman, John Melby, and Raya Orlova.

Some people persisted in criticizing the honesty of Lillian's writing. Nevertheless, most people remember Lillian Hellman for her powerful plays and memoirs, the unforgettable characters she created, and the vital issues she spoke out about with courage and conviction.

Lillian relaxes at her home on Martha's Vineyard.

In 1979 journalist Richard Cohen commented on Lillian in *The Washington Post*. "She has truly become a legend in her own time and one reason is that she has lived long enough to write it herself."

Writing or speaking, Lillian Hellman was never afraid to raise her voice for what she believed. In the history of drama and theater around the world, she will remain one of the most prolific and controversial writers of this or any other century. She will always be the rebel playwright.

Sources

p.7   Lillian Hellman, *An Unfinished Woman,* (Boston: Little, Brown & Co., 1969) 10.

p.15   Ibid., 3.

p.22   Ibid., 27.

p.23   Ibid., 29.

p.25   Ibid., 5.

p.28   Carl Rollyson, *Lillian Hellman: Her Legend and Her Legacy.* (New York: St. Martin's Press, 1988), 27.

p.30   Lillian Hellman, *An Unfinished Woman,* 5.

p.31   Ibid., 31.

p.31   Ibid., 52–53.

p.39   William Wright, *Lillian Hellman: The Image, The Woman* (New York: Simon & Schuster, 1986), 47–48.

p.42   Lillian Hellman, *Scoundrel Time,* (Boston: Little, Brown, & Co., 1976), 41.

p.47   Lillian Hellman, *Days to Come, The Collected Plays of Lillian Hellman,* (Boston, Little, Brown, & Co., 1972), 108.

p.59   Lillian Hellman, *Watch on the Rhine, The Collected Plays of Lillian Hellman,* 254.

p.69   Lillian Hellman, *The Little Foxes, The Collected Plays of Lillian Hellman,* 199.

p.70   Lillian Hellman, *Watch on the Rhine, The Collected Plays of Lillian Hellman,* 264.

p.71   William Wright, *Lillian Hellman: The Image, The Woman,* 168.

p.73   Ibid., 188.

p.76   Lillian Hellman, *An Unfinished Woman,* 153.

p.79   William Wright, *Lillian Hellman: The Image, The Woman,* 209.

p.81   Lillian Hellman, *Scoundrel Time,* 55.

pp.83–84   *The Screen Writer,* December 1947.

p.88   Lillian Hellman, *An Unfinished Woman,* 267–68.

p.91   Lillian Hellman, *Three,* (Boston: Little, Brown, & Co., 1979) 726.

p.95   Lillian Hellman, *Scoundrel Time,* 93.

p.103   Lillian Hellman, *An Unfinished Woman,* 256.

p.107   Ibid., 280.

p.113   William Wright, *Lillian Hellman: The Image, The Woman,* 337.

pp.114–115   Lillian Hellman, *Pentimento,* (Boston: Little, Brown, & Co., 1973), 3.

p.117   Lillian Hellman, *Scoundrel Time,* 155.

p.118   William Wright, *Lillian Hellman: The Image, The Woman,* 378.

p.122   John Hersey, *The Vineyard Gazette,* June 1984.

p.123   Richard Cohen, *The Washington Post,* January 1979.

Bibliography

Writings of Lillian Hellman

The Collected Plays of Lillian Hellman. Boston: Little, Brown, & Co., 1972.

Eating Together: Recollections & Recipes, with Peter Feibleman, Boston: Little, Brown, & Co., 1984.

Maybe. Boston: Little, Brown, & Co., 1980.

Pentimento. Boston: Little, Brown, & Co., 1973.

Scoundrel Time. Boston: Little, Brown, & Co., 1976.

Three. Boston: Little, Brown, & Co., 1979.

An Unfinished Woman. Boston: Little, Brown, & Co., 1969.

Other Sources

Falk, Doris. *Lillian Hellman.* New York: Frederick Ungar, 1978.

Feibleman, Peter. *Lilly.* New York: William Morrow & Co., 1988.

Lederer, Katherine. *Lillian Hellman.* Boston: Twayne, 1979.

Moody, Richard. *Lillian Hellman: Playwright.* Indianapolis: Bobbs-Merrill, 1972.

Rollyson, Carl. *Lillian Hellman: Her Legend and Her Legacy.* New York: St. Martin's Press, 1988.

Towns, Saundra. *Lillian Hellman.* New York: Chelsea House, 1989.

Wright, William. *Lillian Hellman: The Image, The Woman.* New York: Simon & Schuster, 1986.

Index

Photo Acknowledgments

The photographs and illustrations have been reproduced through the courtesy of:
pp. 1, 27 (top), Byron Collection, Museum of the City of New York; pp. 2, 58,
Hearst Newspaper Collection, Special Collections, University of Southern California
Library; pp. 6, 14, the estate of Lillian Hellman; p. 8, Walt Anderson/Visuals
Unlimited; pp. 12 (acc. no. 1950.62.32xvii), 17 (acc. no. 1976.139.25), 18 (acc. no.
1974.25.3.347), 21 (acc. no. 1950.62.32xii), 22 (acc. no. 1959.170.5), The Historic
New Orleans Collection, Museum/Research Center; p. 11, Louisiana Division,
New Orleans Public Library; pp. 24, 90, State Historical Society of Wisconsin; pp. 27
(bottom), 29, United States History, Local History and Geneology Division, New
York Public Library, Astor, Lenox and Tilden Foundations; p. 30, New York
University Archives; p. 32, The Billy Rose Theatre Collection, The New York
Public Library for the Performing Arts, Astor, Lenox and Tilden Foundations; pp.
34, 35, 39, 56, 74, 80, 83 (right), UPI/Bettmann; p. 36, Wisconsin Center for Film
and Theater Research; p. 41, Library of Congress; pp. 44, 48, 49, 64, 66 (both), 68,
78, 84, 89, 102, Photofest; p. 46, photo by Coburn, Museum of the City of New
York, 68.80.1793, Gift of Harold Friedlander; p. 50, Springer/Bettmann Film Archive;
p. 53, Cinema Collectors; p. 54, Hollywood Book and Poster; p. 60, John F. Kennedy
Library; pp. 61, 62, 72, Museum of Modern Art/Film Stills Archives; p. 76, Main
Crimes Commission, National Archives, U.S. Holocaust Memorial Museum; pp. 77,
94, Museum of the City of New York, The Theater Collection; p. 83 (left), Office of
War Information, National Archives, photo no. 208-PS-50-5171; p. 85, State Historical
Society of Iowa, Iowa City; pp. 86, 106, 113, 116, UPI/Bettmann Newsphotos; p. 93,
The Bettmann Archives; pp. 96, 100, 101, 108, 114, Boston Public Library, Print
Department; p. 97, U.S. Senate Historical Office; p. 105, Smithsonian Institution;
p. 109, Smith College Archives; p. 110, National Archives, photo no. 306-SS-28B-35-6;
p. 118, Collector's Bookstore; p. 119, Harcourt Brace Jovanovich; p. 123, Alison
Shaw. Front and back cover photographs courtesy of Photofest.